SILENT HATTIE SPEAKS

Contributions in Women's Studies

The Chains of Protection: The Judicial Response to Women's Labor Legislation
Judith A. Baer

Women's Studies: An Interdisciplinary Collection
Kathleen O'Connor Blumhagen and Walter D. Johnson, editors

Latin American Women: Historical Perspectives
Asunción Lavrin

Beyond Her Sphere: Women and the Professions in American History
Barbara J. Harris

Literary America, 1903-1934: The Mary Austin Letters
T. M. Pearce, editor

The American Woman in Transition: The Urban Influence, 1870-1920
Margaret Gibbons Wilson

Liberators of the Female Mind: The Shirreff Sisters, Educational Reform, and the Women's Movement
Edward W. Ellsworth

The Jewish Feminist Movement in Germany: The Campaigns of the Jüdischer Frauenbund, 1904-1938
Marion A. Kaplan

SILENT HATTIE SPEAKS

The Personal Journal of Senator Hattie Caraway

Edited by
Diane D. Kincaid

Contributions in Women's Studies, Number 9

Greenwood Press
Westport, Connecticut • London, England

Library of Congress Cataloging in Publication Data

Caraway, Hattie Wyatt, 1878-
    Silent Hattie speaks.

    (Contributions in women's studies ; no. 9 ISSN 0147-104X)
    Bibliography: p.
    Includes index.
    1. Caraway, Hattie Wyatt, 1878-   2. Legislators—
United States—Biography. 3. United States. Congress.
Senate-Biography. I. Kincaid, Diane D. II. Title.
III. Series.
E748.C228A34   328.73'092'4 [B]   78-22136
ISBN 0-313-20820-4

Library of Congress Catalog Card Number: 78-22136
ISBN: 0-313-20820-4
ISSN: 0147-104X

First published in 1979

Greenwood Press, Inc.
51 Riverside Avenue, Westport, Connecticut 06880

Printed in the United States of America
10 9 8 7 6 5 4 3 2 1

Contents

Illustrations

Acknowledgments

During the course of my research, I received invaluable assistance from many kind people. Among those who were exceptionally generous with their time and memories were Paul and Della Caraway, Joe Martin, Bill Penix, and Brooks Hays. Bobby Roberts, Sam Sizer, and Ethel Simpson of the Special Collections Department of the University of Arkansas Library at Fayetteville and Elizabeth G. Wittlake, assistant curator of the Arkansas State University Museum at Jonesboro, were extremely helpful. I received excellent research assistance from JoAnn Nash, Heather Blair, and my mother, Minna R. Divers, who is fortuitously located on Capitol Hill. Pictures and original material were generously provided by Fred Huston of Oklahoma City and John Wells of Little Rock. Jo Wheeler of Jonesboro provided me with a real home away from home. Professor Margaret Bolsterli supplied the original idea, and Professor Willard B. Gatewood, Jr., encouraged me to pursue it. My children, Bill and Kathryn, allowed me many hours that otherwise would have been theirs.

I
INTRODUCTION

For a brief period in the early 1930s, Hattie Caraway was one of the most visible women in America. The first woman elected to the United States Senate, she was the subject of numerous newspaper stories and interviews, and each of her breakthrough achievements (the first woman to vote in the Senate, to preside over the Senate, to chair a Senate committee, to preside over Senate hearings) precipitated another spurt of publicity. When she left the Senate in 1944, however, running a poor fourth in an election that elevated J. William Fulbright to her seat, this defeat and subsequent departure received little attention. Her death in 1950 was scarcely noted in the national press.

The recent resurgence of American feminism has created considerable interest in those few women who have been politically prominent, and seemingly should have turned considerable attention to one of only fourteen women to have served in the Senate. To date, however, the spotlight has not returned to Hattie Caraway.

Perhaps conventional characterizations of Sen. Caraway have been such to disinterest and disappoint contemporary feminists, inasmuch as she has been generally depicted as a wholly apolitical woman who "inherited" her husband's Senate seat when he died in office and secured her first reelection only through the vigorous intervention of Sen. Huey P. Long—two paths to power that may seem more of an embarrassment than an inspiration to the present-day push for more women in public office.[1] Furthermore some of the statements most frequently, and sometimes falsely, attributed to her have the distinct ring of heresy in many modern ears. Speaking of her original appointment, for example, she is supposed to have said, "Dad wouldn't like it. He was dead set against women in politics."[2]

Small wonder, then, that few have been eager to revive the original interest in Hattie Caraway and that Hattie Caraway has become a name that is vaguely familiar attached to a person who is not. In February 1978, one national newsman covering Muriel Humphrey's Senate swearing-in ceremony referred to "Cattie Haraway" as the first woman to have succeeded her deceased husband to the Senate. In March 1978, a candidate announced for the United States Senate from Arkansas saying he had wanted to make the race ever since following "John L. McClellan's winning campaign over Hattie Caraway in 1942," an astonishing source of inspiration since it was Sen. Caraway who defeated John McClellan with 51.2 percent of the vote in 1938.[3]

To quote Sen. Caraway herself, from her journal, "Of what things is fame made? 'Thank God I too shall die.'"[4] No amount of revisionism can, or should, rehabilitate Sen. Caraway as a forceful legislative leader. She was not. She was, however, as her journal demonstrates, a much stronger, more complicated, and more interesting woman than has been generally supposed.

HATTIE W. CARAWAY

Hattie Ophelia Wyatt was born on February 1, 1878, near Bakerville, Tennessee.[5] In 1882 the family moved to nearby Hustburg, Tennessee, where Hattie grew up doing chores on the family farm and helping out in her father's general store. At age fifteen she enrolled in the Dickson (Tennessee) Normal College, perhaps better termed an academy, from which she graduated with a B.A. degree in 1896.

While at Dickson, she became engaged to fellow student Thaddeus Horatio Caraway, who had been earning his education as a cotton picker, sawmill laborer, and railway section hand. After graduation, both Hattie and Thad taught school for several years, while he also pursued a law degree. In 1902 they were married and settled in Jonesboro, Arkansas. Hattie bore two sons, Paul Wyatt and Forrest, and tended to them, the house, and garden while Thad began pursuing both a political and a legal career.

He was elected prosecuting attorney in 1908 and United States congressman in 1912. The Caraways moved to Washington, D.C., where a third son, Robert Easley, was born. In 1920, the first election in which Hattie could vote (pursuant to the Nineteenth Amendment), Thad was elected to the Senate, where he built

Hattie Caraway with young sons Forrest and Paul, c. 1911. Courtesy of Fred Huston.

a reputation as a champion of the poor white farmers of his state and region, a foe of lobbyists, a die-hard Democrat, and a fierce opponent in debate. Known as "Fighting Thad" to his friends and "Caustic Caraway" to his enemies, he was reelected to the Senate in 1926 and was making plans to seek another term in 1932. On November 6, 1931, while recuperating from what had seemed to be successful kidney stone surgery, however, he suddenly developed a blood clot and died. While the widow and sons grieved, and friends worried about the family's financial situation, the state's politicians faced a sticky problem.[6]

Under Arkansas law, had Thad died three days later (leaving less than a year until the next general election), the governor could have simply appointed someone to serve out the remainder of the term; and this option was at first considered. It soon became clear, however, that although a brief interim appointment was legally possible—and was being pressed for by Senate Democrats, Thad's death having restored a plurality to the Republicans—a special election would be necessary for the bulk of the remaining term.[7]

Although other candidates were considered, most of those eyeing the 1932 Senate race quickly agreed with Gov. Harvey Parnell that naming Thad's widow as interim appointee, and as the Democratic party's nominee in the obligatory special election, was the most generally acceptable choice. It ensured that none of the potential candidates would have the advantages of incumbency in the 1932 race; nor would anyone risk offending voters' sensibilities by seeming to have manipulated his way into office. Furthermore there was ample Arkansas precedent for the widow of a deceased member of Congress serving as "benchwarmer": Pearl Oldfield had been elected to fill out Rep. William Oldfield's term in 1929, and Effiegene Wingo had been elected to serve out Rep. John Wingo's term in 1930.

Amid general praise for the graciousness of the gesture and political shrewdness of the decision, Gov. Parnell made the interim appointment on November 13, 1931. Hattie Caraway returned to Washington where, on December 9, 1931, she was sworn into office as a United States Senator. While the fifty-three-year-old widow began settling into her new responsibilities (and keeping a journal), Gov. Parnell was discovering that securing her desired nomination by the Democratic State Committee as the party's candidate in the special election he had called for January 12, 1932, was not going to be unopposed.

Frank Pace, who had been a law partner of former Arkansas governor Jeff Davis, made a determined effort to obtain the committee's nomination for himself, and he came close to succeeding. However, with the help of those wanting to protect their own potential Senate candidacies (primarily Gov. Parnell but also Rep. Heartsill Ragon) and with a last-minute lobbying boost from Jonesboro friends and politicians (who actually set up headquarters in Little Rock's Marion Hotel for the undertaking), the committee nominated Hattie Caraway as their candidate on December 2, 1931.[8]

In thoroughly Democratic Arkansas, Sen. Caraway's ability to defeat the two men who filed as "Independents" (Sam Carson, a farmer of Detonti, and Rex Floyd, son of the late Rep. J. C. Floyd of Yellville) was never seriously in doubt. What was in doubt, and raised serious problems for a while, were the logistics of the election itself. Primaries in Arkansas were (and still are) financed primarily through filing fees paid by the numerous candidates; and county officials immediately let Gov. Parnell know that they could not afford to hold what was seen as an essentially pro forma election because there would not be sufficient funds to pay the necessary judges and clerks. What occurred then is an interesting footnote in feminist, as well as Arkansas, history.

The male political establishment presented the problem of no funds to finance the election as "a challenge to Arkansas womanhood."[9] As one politician pointed out, in patronizing but effective terms, if the women wanted the privilege of having one of their own sex in the United States Senate, then they must "show their appreciation with a bit of personal sacrifice" to avoid "the disgrace of the election going by default."[10]

The challenge seems to have been accepted with gusto. The Democratic State Committee named a special seven-woman committee to turn out the female vote on January 12 (and a separate all-male committee to "insure that voters don't lose interest in the election"); and the Women's City Club of Little Rock formed the Arkansas Women's Democratic Club specifically for the purpose of insuring adequate numbers of volunteer election officials.[11] The latter group devised schemes for increasing voter turnout, made speeches before civic clubs and political meetings, raised money for and mounted an advertising campaign, offered voters rides to the polls, and eventually found a sufficient number of volunteer election officials, primarily women, in seventy-two of the state's seventy-five counties.

Despite newspaper predictions that the expected rain "would have even greater effect than usual because mainly it is women who have expressed interest in this race," and some male disgruntlement ("A husband used to be able to go home after work to a nice hot meal. Now a man's got to wait until the election is over to take the judge home"), the election was a splendid success.[12]

Hattie Caraway received 31,133 votes to Rex Floyd's 1,752. Sam Carson with 1,095 did not carry even his county. Women, serving the purposes of male politicians, had elected a woman to the Senate. The men may have later regretted setting this force loose upon the political scene: within a year's time the Arkansas Women's Democratic Club was discussing plans for full representation of women on state and county committees and requesting equal patronage.

For the moment, however, the political establishment's ship was back on course. While Sen. Caraway continued familiarizing herself with office routine, committee work, and parliamentary procedure, some of the state's most prominent politicians proceeded to announce their candidacies and plan their campaigns for what they presumed would be a vacated seat.

On May 10, 1932—the last day before the filing deadline for the August 10 Democratic primary—these men were momentarily distracted when a special delivery letter arrived from Washington containing Sen. Caraway's filing fee and party pledge. Although the newspapers had a brief field-day, ("Bombshell Explodes in Arkansas Politics," "Jonesboro Senator Springs Surprise by Announcing for Office"), the six men who had also filed simply

continued with their own campaigns, convinced that Sen. Caraway was not a serious contender.[13]

At the time, the assumption seemed sound. Caraway had no
campaign funds, no campaign manager, no campaign plans, and
not a single political leader came forward to back her.[14] By contrast, all six of her opponents had fairly impressive credentials:
O. L. Bodenhamer, an El Dorado businessman, had been national
commander of the American Legion; Charles Brough was an
economics lecturer at the University of Arkansas and a former
governor; William Hutton was secretary of the State Democratic
Committee, a former football star, and Pulaski County sheriff;
William Kirby was an associate justice of the Arkansas Supreme
Court and a former United States Senator; Vincent Miles had
been Democratic National Committeeman for seventeen years;
and Melbourne Martin was a lawyer with sufficient funds to do
the most extensive newspaper advertising.

There was somewhat more concern when, on July 19, Sen.
Caraway announced that Sen. Huey P. Long of Louisiana was going to come to Arkansas to help place her record before the
people; but when July ended with still no signs of real activity in
the Caraway camp, it was widely predicted that she would receive
no more than 3,000 of an estimated 300,000 votes to be cast.[15]

On August 1, Sen. Long roared into Arkansas in a long, black
limousine accompanied by an entourage that included two trucks
wired with loudspeakers and rooftop platforms for makeshift
speakers' stands, four vans transporting campaign posters and
literature, and a number of helpful and energetic young men on
"temporary leave" from the Louisiana Highway Department.[16]
The mechanics were stupenduous: part of the traveling campaign camp tore ahead to attract crowds and make arrangements
in the next town while the two senators made their pitch to the
immense throngs previously gathered. The message was unmis-
takable: Sen. Caraway had bravely and consistently stood by the
common people. Sen. Long appealed to his listeners' chivalry
("We're here to pull a lot of pot-bellied politicians off a little
woman's neck"), economic resentments ("If we can't win on her
record we might as well turn the government over to the corporations"), and provincial pride ("Oh, if you defeat her, the big

metropolitan papers will praise you. They'll say that the electorate of Arkansas is enlightened and intelligent. Yes, yes — if you'll
cut your throat for them, they'll drink your blood, and they will
give you sweet words as long as you vote yourselves further into
slavery.")[17] Hattie herself spoke only briefly, but in the same vein
of appeal, to the depression-stricken farmers: "I have observed
the Farm Board members testifying before the Senate Agriculture Committee and they did not know how many elevators and
warehouses the Farm Board was operating but they always have
beautifully manicured fingernails."[18]

When Sen. Long left the state one week later, he and Sen.
Caraway had traveled two thousand miles, been to thirty-one
counties, made thirty-nine speeches, and personally reached
over 200,000 people. By midweek Sen. Caraway's opponents
became seriously alarmed. Brough and Bodenhamer attacked
Sen. Long; Kirby turned his fury on Sen. Caraway herself. Still
nobody correctly predicted the final outcome: Hattie Caraway
received 127,702 votes, 44.7 percent of all those cast, carrying
sixty-one of Arkansas's seventy-five counties. Assured of the
Democratic nomination, and therefore of general election victory in November, a woman had been elected to a full six-year
term in the United States Senate for the first time.[19]

The election was the most dramatic episode in Sen. Caraway's
career. It was by no means the end of it. For the next six years,
she devoted herself quietly to her Senate work. She rarely made
public statements but strongly supported almost all of President
Roosevelt's New Deal legislative program, helped find jobs for
many seeking employment in the difficult depression years, and
actively assisted many Arkansas communities in securing numerous grants and loans for assorted public works projects.

Many assumed she would announce her retirement before the
1938 Senate contest, but again she confounded the political
prophets by filing for reelection. Huey Long, who had been assas-
sinated on September 8, 1935, was no longer available to assist
her. She had, however, the powerful backing of Homer Adkins,
then Collector of Internal Revenue, later governor of Arkansas,
and also received a mild endorsement from President Roosevelt,
which she strongly exploited. With additional support from orga-

nized labor, veterans, and women's groups, she narrowly defeated Rep. John McClellan (whose slogan was "Arkansas needs another man in the Senate") by eight thousand votes.[20]

Sen. Caraway's last six years in the Senate were much like the preceding seven. She continued to be one of President Roosevelt's most faithful Senate supporters. She saw that constituents' requests were promptly and adequately answered. She assisted with a successful effort to block a lessening of Arkansas's representation in Congress in 1941 and continued to work with the Arkansas delegation in securing beneficial public works for the state.

Like many other politicians, however, she failed to recognize that her methods were growing outdated, her popularity and support declining; and many of her friends were dismayed when she insisted on running again in 1944. The decision was a mistake. She was badly beaten in the Democratic primary.

Sen Caraway finished her public career by accepting an appointment from President Roosevelt to the Employees Compensation Commission, later to the Employees Compensation Appeals Board. At age seventy-two she suffered a severe stroke and died on December 22, 1950.

THE JOURNAL

Shortly after Hattie Caraway was sworn in as Senator, she began to keep a daily record on United States Senate stationery. The first entry was made on December 14, 1931, and notations continue quite regularly until late May 1932, when they begin declining in both length and regularity, fading out in midsentence on June 9. She briefly resumed the journal in January 1934 but after a few entries ceased altogether.

What is published here is complete in the sense that it is a verbatim reproduction of everything that is known to exist of Hattie Caraway's journal, incomplete in that it covers only part of one of her thirteen years in the Senate.[21] Because it is a fragment, and because much of that fragment will inevitably seem frivolous, it is important to try to understand why she kept it and what it can tell us that is not already known.

With respect to Sen. Caraway's motives in keeping this chronicle, there are several possibilities. The most obvious would be that same combination of purposes that prompts many public officials to keep a private record. Most public actors are anxious to receive a favorable, or at least fair, rating on their performances, and a journal can be useful in securing such a verdict. It is a way of tracking one's own role in and perspective on important contemporary developments for future purposes.

It is clear that Sen. Caraway had some intentions that this journal eventually be made public. She occasionally notes that a particular thought or poem is "copied here to preserve for the world."[22] Once after expressing some particularly venomous thoughts about Arkansas's senior senator, Joseph T. Robinson, she writes, "This is pretty personal little journal, but I will edit before its published—if ever." She then adds, in a delighted afterthought, "Doesn't it sound big to think or talk of having something published?"[23] When she notes in her last entry, "Here on March 28th 1934 I want to inscribe in this journal the account of the only time the President has talked to me in the interest of any measure that was at all close in the Senate," her intent is clearly within the usual journal tradition.[24] She wants to be sure that her version of particular events eventually would be known and understood.

If Sen. Caraway's major purpose was preserving her version of history for posterity, it must be acknowledged that she is not particularly successful in achieving it. The journal begins in a year when the true terrors of the depression were becoming evident: the stock market had collapsed, banks had failed, commodity prices had slipped, numerous mortgages had been foreclosed, unemployment had soared, breadlines had formed, and many Americans were growing radical and riotous. In the United States Senate, raging legislative battles, reflecting profound philosophical differences, were daily being waged over the appropriate governmental response. These debates are referred to by Sen. Caraway but more as background than for content. Those seeking greater insight into the Senate's reaction to (and neglect of) the decaying economy will have to look elsewhere.[25]

Sen. Caraway's characterizations of individuals are only somewhat more successful than her descriptions of events. The Senate at this time was populated with genuine giants, men whose names were then or later became universally familiar: Alben Barkley, Hugo Black, William Borah, James F. Byrnes, Cordell Hull, Arthur Vandenberg. They all appear in Sen. Caraway's journal; the descriptive references are sometimes interesting and occasionally amusing, but our understanding of these notables is not significantly deepened by her observations.

Why, if she was at least considering eventual publication, did she not put into her journal more appropriate material? Possibly she was too naive, or at least inexperienced, to know what kinds of data give such journals their value. Possibly she was too far from the real center of Senate decision making to give us a genuinely inside view. Or, still within the journal tradition but with a less noble twist, possibly she was motivated not so much by the verdict of posterity as by the hope of profit. This possibility is suggested not only by the contemporary example of some famous practitioners but even more by our knowledge that this thought was planted in Sen. Caraway's mind by a family friend and financial adviser, E. J. Bodman, at the time of her original appointment. Bodman, knowing that Sen. Thad Caraway had left little to his widow but some heavily mortgaged property, encouraged Hattie not only to serve out Thad's term in the Senate, for which she would be paid ten thousand dollars, but also to exploit that unique experience afterward. Specifically he recalled advising her to "employ a publicity man to keep a diary for her with the idea of selling it after completing her term."[26] With this suggestion in mind, she might well have assumed that the journal would have interest because a woman had kept it and that a "woman's eye" view of the Senate (how senators dressed, what the ladies said at lunch) would be its major sales appeal.

The existence of some profit motive would also help to explain why she later abandoned the journal. By August 1932, Sen. Caraway had been assured of an additional six years in the Senate. Perhaps also by this time she had acquired sufficient sophistication to know that much of what she had recorded as a freshman senator (endless descriptions of her colleagues' costumes and speaking mannerisms, family visits, luncheon menus) was of little real interest. The last few entries in 1934 are much more compatible with the usual journal tradition than much of what precedes them.

Quite distinctive from the journal tradition, but presenting a whole range of other possible motives, is what might be called the diary tradition. Journals, papers, and memoirs usually record one's personal participation in worldly affairs. Diaries have traditionally recorded the movements of one's mind and emotions. Journals are usually intended to enter the public domain; diaries quite frequently are meant to perish with their author. Because men, until recently, have been the predominant movers and shapers of public events, journal keeping has been primarily a masculine, and somewhat elitist, tradition; for millions of women, at some critical points or throughout their lives, the keeping of a diary has been a profoundly important, but altogether private, occupation.

In an introduction to a recently published collection of diaries of women, M. J. Moffat mentions a great variety of diary-keeping motivations, all of which are applicable in Sen. Caraway's circumstances: a safe outlet for emotion, psychological alienation from one's milieu, confusion about conflicting demands, a reminder of one's self-significance, the necessity for a trusted confidante.[27] Sen. Caraway describes what she writes as her "little journal," but what she writes falls more clearly into the diary than the journal category.[28]

Whatever the original intent may have been for this document, it seems to have become something much more private than public, a place where the brave front displayed to the outside world could be discarded. For example, when Sen. Caraway is unexpectedly called upon to preside over the Senate, she blithely tells a reporter that "there was nothing to it," but later she tells her journal, "I was scared." She mentally faults a colleague's high-handedness when in her judgment compromise was called for, but notes to her journal, "Oh, well, a woman on suffrance here may only think, and put in a private journal any thoughts she may have."[29]

Nowhere is the use of the diary as confidante more evident, or more illuminating, than in her extended agonizing over whether to run for reelection. She wants sound advice but senses that nobody in a position to give it is disinterested. "I have had to be so alone, so very close-mouthed," she writes, "that mayhap my chances are not so good. I'm so afraid my judgment is so warped by my desires in the matter that I cannot come happily to any decision."[30]

Since all we can do regarding her purposes is speculate, I would suggest that the journal was probably begun as an eventual source of income but that this rationale became increasingly subordinate to others: the pleasure of writing, an antidote to boredom, an outlet for vexation, a source of self-satisfaction, and, especially, a trusted confessor and companion in an atmosphere perceived as unsympathetic and untrustworthy.

Whatever Sen. Caraway's conscious purposes may have been, what unconsciously seems to emerge are two quite different stories. One is the account of a woman, serving as no other woman had previously done, in the United States Senate. This woman is often intimidated, sometimes exasperated, but frequently exhilarated by the abundant attentions newly accorded to her. She is given awards, sought out by photographers, fussed and fawned over. She continues her faithful attendance at the Tuesday Senate ladies' luncheons but is now given a seat of honor. "A little difference in status makes more difference to more people than I had realized," she notes.[31]

The other story is that of a woman who dearly loved her husband, attempting to adjust to life without him. She sadly notes their wedding anniversary and the monthly anniversaries of his death. Another senator's worn suit reminds her of "Dad," as does his favorite anti-Hoover joke, and there are occasional tears when an old photograph or another death forces her feelings to the surface. She constantly frets over finances, worrying about "the years and years of dependence one may have to endure." The presence of one son at home, two others close by, a sister and other relatives, a steady stream of visitors, does not fill the gap left by Thad's absence. "No one," she writes "will ever know how much we miss him."[32]

Both stories, of course, emerge from the same event—Thad Caraway's death—which means that each new accolade, each

Hattie Caraway with her husband, Sen. Thaddeus Caraway. Library of Congress.

acknowledgment of status, is both a source of satisfaction and a painful reminder of loss. After an angry confrontation with a job-seeking woman, Sen. Caraway writes, "I would rather have him back than any job in the world," and there is no doubt that is so. Yet the job certainly helps to pass the days and ease the pain.[33]

Hattie sometimes seems concerned that her involvement in, and enjoyment of, her new activities shows disrespect for the husband she once so willingly served as helpmate, and occasionally there is the shadow of guilt. "I can but think—I did not try to wear the pants while Dad lived," she muses, "yet I'm trying to fit my feet into his shoes." Quickly, however, a comforting rationalization follows the self-doubts: "I can well know they are easier on my feet than they'd be on Parnell's or Kirby's."[34]

If the journal is uneven, it reflects not only the conflicting purposes of the author but the emotional and logical inconsistencies of her position. To date, all but one of the fourteen women who have served in the Senate first entered to fill a vacancy, twelve of which were created by death. Half of all women elected to the United States House of Representatives have been widows at the time they took office, most having replaced their deceased husbands.[35]

We do not know, of course, whether the kinds of conflicting emotions that Hattie Caraway articulates are characteristic of those who have obtained a prestigious political position as a consequence of their husband's death. It is possible, however, that Sen. Caraway's journal illuminates more than her own individual experience—that it speaks for and about other women whose political success has been inseparable from personal loss and grief. This in itself would give the journal value.

Even more important, however, is the new perspectives the journal offers on the three subjects on which there has been the widest divergence of opinion: Caraway's surprising decision to run for reelection in 1932, her relationship with Sen. Huey P. Long, and the true nature of this "conspicuously inconspicuous" person.[36] It is disappointing, of course, that the journal covers only the first of Sen. Caraway's thirteen years in the Senate. It was in that first year however, when the events giving rise to the first two of these controversies arose; and fragmentary as it is, the thoughts Hattie herself recorded sometimes confirm, but often confound, the image created by the thousands of words once written about her.

THE DECISION TO RUN

It is impossible to overemphasize the universality of the belief that Hattie Caraway would step aside quietly after filling out her late husband's unexpired term. Virtually everything surrounding her entry into the Senate pointed toward a speedy exit. Her assumed departure, after all, was her primary appeal to the various politicians, especially Gov. Parnell, who overcame opposition to secure the office for her. Every news story surrounding her appointment not only candidly discussed this angle but usually went on to name those who would be contenders when the seat was vacated.[37]

From the beginning, those closest to Caraway gave every indication that she would be precisely the compliant benchwarmer the state's politicians wanted. They emphasized her extreme reluctance to accept even the brief interim appointment; and especially when Frank Pace's efforts to secure the Democratic Party's nomination began to threaten her candidacy seriously, her supporters rushed to assure the press that she "would not seek the office for the full term."[38]

Journalists embellished the theme: "If she had her own wish, she would retire from the limelight and devote her life to a mother's care for her three young sons." If anyone wondered whether twenty-two- and twenty-six-year-old West Point graduates, and one high school senior, needed that much mother's care, there were statements attributed directly to one of the sons in question. Paul Caraway was quoted as saying that his mother did not care to enter politics and that no member of the family was "politically minded."[39]

Hattie Caraway never made any such explicit public disclaimer herself, but had there been any doubts of her intentions, other factors would have resolved them.[40] Two wives of deceased Arkansas congressmen had recently taken seats in the House of Representatives under similar circumstances, and neither Pearl

Oldfield nor Effiegene Wingo attempted to extend her tenure in office.

Hattie Caraway was a woman, a southern woman, and southern women were invariably expected to serve as auxiliaries to, not competitors against, their dominant men.[41] In collecting material for this volume, I interviewed many men, all of whom said they were surprised, astonished, shocked when Sen. Caraway announced she would seek election to the full term. A female friend of Sen. Caraway's said that she was not. "But virtually all of the politicians I've talked to were dumbfounded," I pointed out. "Of course," she replied. "They are all men."[42]

Finally, it must be pointed out that many of those close to the situation believed that Sen. Caraway was not only politically obligated to Gov. Parnell for his efforts in her behalf but that she had personally and explicitly promised him that—if appointed and nominated—she would attempt to go no further. Was such a promise made and then broken? Certainly Gov. Parnell thought he had a commitment and told others such a promise had been specifically made.[43] Harry Lee Williams' angry assertion that there had been a clear commitment and that Parnell "received the double-cross" is so emotional as to be suspect;[44] but others are as convinced as Williams that a promise came not just from the Caraway camp but from Caraway herself.[45] In fact, according to one affidavit, the pact was sealed in the presence of one of Hattie Caraway's sons, with the promise of generous financial support to Parnell in his Senate campaign, in return for his appointing and securing the party nomination for Hattie.[46]

Others insist that though many of Caraway's friends and supporters were pressured to make such a promise,[47] and some may have done so in her behalf, Hattie Caraway herself neither made nor authorized any such commitment.[48] In fact, her son Paul specifically recollects her silence: "I can still see her in the rocking-chair in the front room as all the politicians came to call. She rocked and rocked, but she didn't say anything."[49]

There is something almost ludicrous, and logically inconsistent, about all these politicians seeking so strenuously for a promise to step down from a woman who was simultaneously being characterized as a wholly domestic woman who wanted no part of public life. The Parnell political apparatus, however, was both tough and determined; and perhaps they had some slight suspicions that Caraway was not going to be as cooperative as the public generally assumed.[50]

One of the most valuable aspects of the journal is the light it sheds on this controversy. It reveals, in the first place, that almost from the beginning of her tenure, Sen. Caraway was strongly attracted to and seriously considering the possibility of running again. By February 24, she is already agonizing and reproving herself to "try not to dwell on what I'd *like* to do." Also from the beginning she senses that her candidacy would be extremely unpopular with her congressional colleagues and that she must be very guarded in what she tells them.[51] By February 29, she is methodically sizing up the potential opposition. It also becomes apparent that although the press, the public, and many politicians were caught entirely off guard by her eventual announcement that she would run, some insiders had begun to grow suspicious, hence the steady stream of inquiries noted in her journal, to all of which she is noncommittal.[52]

Most significant are Sen. Caraway's own repeated assertions to her journal that she is under no obligation to Gov. Parnell. When she is dunned for a printing bill, she peevishly dismisses any implications that nonpayment would show her ingratitude to Parnell. When Parnell contacts her for support on a federal judgeship, she refuses to commit. And, anticipating that should she run, the charge of ingratitude will be made, she specifically and vigorously refutes it: "Parnell can not claim any promise from me for none of his efforts to buy me succeeded." Somewhat enigmatically the entry continues, "I refused to make any promises and I can't forgive his heartlessness and the mental agony he must have caused Dad those last days."[53] What this suggests is that Sen. Caraway not only felt no gratitude toward Gov. Parnell but strongly resented him for some insult, real or imagined, to her deceased husband and therefore to herself.

No entirely satisfactory explanation for this resentment has been forthcoming. Hattie was furious about being approached by one potential successor to her husband, seeking her endorsement for his candidacy within thirty minutes of Thad's death.[54]

But there is no indication that this insensitive and overly eager aspirant was Parnell nor would that explain Parnell's alleged "heartlessness" to Thad Caraway while he still lived.

Perhaps Thad, knowing the serious nature of his surgery and the poor state of his finances, attempted to elicit a promise from Parnell that Hattie would be named to succeed him should the worst happen. If Parnell were noncommittal, and especially if Thad had communicated this state of affairs to Hattie, that would explain not only her own determined silence but her later resentment.

This interpretation, admittedly, is entirely speculative, and some mystery remains. In all, however, it is clear that Sen. Caraway felt no obligation to Parnell, in fact, felt justified in deliberately thwarting him. In her own bitter words, "I won't be the first woman who has been sacrificed to the ambition of some man."[55]

Having finally struggled to and announced her decision to seek another term, what the journal then catalogs is a brief period of postdecision euphoria ("If I can hold on to my sense of humor and a modicum of dignity I shall have had a wonderful time running for office, whether I get there or not") followed by profound disillusionment bordering on depression ("I'm in for crucifixion").[56]

The journal entries become shorter and less regular, with frequent references to her being tired and cross. The journal, as well as her political career, might well have been reaching its conclusion, except for the timely intervention of Sen. Huey P. Long.

HUEY LONG AND THE 1932 CAMPAIGN

Even more surprising than Sen. Caraway's decision to seek re-election was her eventual victory. There is some difference of opinion as to whether this triumph was due wholly, or only partially, to Sen. Huey Long's whirlwind campaign in her behalf, but nobody has claimed she could have succeeded without him.[57] As Sen. Caraway herself publicly acknowledged, his assistance was the decisive factor.[58] What has been debated, and variously interpreted, is why Sen. Long came to her assistance and on what terms. Here, too, the journal provides some important insights. It certainly refutes any later claims that Sen. Long persuaded Sen.

Caraway to make the race;[59] she had made that decision, and acted upon it, well before he offered to help.[60]

The usual interpretation is that Sen. Long chose to intervene in Sen. Caraway's campaign for a number of politically self-enhancing reasons. Emerging triumphant in a race generally conceded to be hopeless would dramatize his political appeal to a national audience and demonstrate that his power extended beyond Louisiana. Furthermore it offered an excellent opportunity to embarrass, and perhaps intimidate, Sen. Joseph T. Robinson of Arkansas, Democratic minority leader, against whom Sen. Long had mounted a furiously critical campaign. Finally Sen. Long was probably interested in retaining one of the few senators who shared at least some of his convictions, Sen. Caraway even having dared to vote for his proposal limiting individual incomes to one million dollars a year.[61]

It has also been suggested that Sen. Long's numerous selfish motives were reinforced by sentiment. Sen. Burton K. Wheeler has related a story, told to him by Sen. Long, of Long's having been moved to assist by the widow's tears.[62] T. Harry Williams, Long's major biographer, has conceded that Long was a sentimentalist as well as an opportunist and that a modicum of sympathy may well have been involved. Primarily, however, Williams insists that Long was "moving with his customary calculation" in taking over Sen. Caraway's floundering campaign.[63] Nothing in the journal refutes these conventional explanations of Sen. Long's interest in Sen. Caraway's campaign. What the journal does provide is Sen. Caraway's perspective, which seems to have been remarkably similar to his: political need reinforced by personal attachment.

From Sen. Caraway's point of view, Sen. Long's late arrival in the Senate (self-delayed to insure that an unfriendly lieutenant governor did not replace him) was immensely welcome for a number of reasons. She recalls the affection and admiration her deceased husband had for him and eagerly anticipates that he will enliven Senate proceedings with "color and quite a display of fireworks."[64] Although she is sometimes embarrassed by Long's crude manners and verbal excesses, she applauds his ability to articulate the impatience she feels with the Senate's snail-pace deliberations while people are going hungry.

Hattie Caraway with Sen. Huey P. Long, August 1931. Louisiana State University Archives.

We know from the journal how frequently she felt bored, intimidated, and lonely. It is not surprising that "Huey, the dynamic Governor," quickly becomes a bright spot. From the day he is sworn in, she begins to note his frequent absences and welcome his exuberant returns. Once she tells her journal, with obvious delight, that Huey had "asked how his pardner was and whether she was true to the Kingfish."[65]

Clearly both senators were engaged in some deliberate cultivation: Long bolsters her morale by voting with her; she lavishes praise on him for a speech that, she tells her journal, was "perfectly *mad*."[66] Generally, however, their camaraderie seems to have been the genuine outgrowth of the populistic philosophy they shared and of the position of being outsiders that they mutually occupied.

If there is such a thing as a Senate Club, neither Long nor Caraway were—or ever could have been—members: Long because of his loud voice, bizarre appearance, controversial career, radical ideas; Caraway because she was a woman. Both knew they were not welcome; and seated together on the last row, these two embarrassments to the establishment seem to have formed their own backbenchers' society where they could swap jokes, trade news, bolster each other's self-esteem, and worry about the other one's political future. If she was "this brave little woman" to him, he was "poor lamb" to her.[67]

On both sides, then, there was genuine affection. For both, however, personal friendship was secondary to political ambition. Long's offer to assist Caraway was undoubtedly motivated primarily by his own power motives. Her acceptance of that offer came from her desire to win. Her journal clearly shows that whatever illusions she may have had about her viability as a candidate were soon shattered. "Woe, woe, woe," she writes; and later, "Guess I'm a goat all right."[68]

In these circumstances, Sen. Long's surprise offer of assistance on May 21 must have seemed like a godsend, especially since prior to that time she had noted, "I know I've had no offers of help from any political leader." Apparently, however, realizing there might be dangerous strings attached, she refused, or postponed, accepting the offer: "I can't sell my soul and live with myself. It would mean nothing to me to sit here day after day and have no freedom of voting."[69] This is her last journal reference to Sen. Long, and without any evidence to the contrary, it would be fair to conclude that she eventually rationalized "selling her soul" as the price of victory. But this does not seem to have happened.

By many later accounts, including her own, when she finally agreed to accept his intervention, it was on two firm conditions: that he not use her campaign as an excuse for attacking Joseph T. Robinson in Arkansas and that he could not expect to control her vote in the future.[70] Judging by the public record, both commitments were honored.

Although Long's virulent criticism of the Wall Street power interests and what he called their political stooges clearly included Robinson in its sweep, he steadfastly refused, even under provocation, to name Robinson directly;[71] and Sen. Caraway's subsequent voting record was much more pro-Roosevelt than pro-Long.[72] On the one known occasion when Long specifically asked for her support, a vote with him against the World Court, she refused.[73] The relationship, then, seems to have been not one of unilateral exploitation by Sen. Long of a naive woman but one of mutual admiration, mutual protection, and mutual political advantage.

SILENT HATTIE

The circumstances surrounding Hattie Caraway's entry into the Senate produced some highly contradictory publicity. While newspapers were assuring their readers that "she is a homeloving woman and glad to escape the responsibilities of public life," they were also advising that beneath that modest exterior was "a keen mind," "a sparkling wit," and "a wide knowledge of the workings of national politics and government."[74]

Some of the original descriptions of her capabilities were probably exaggerated for a purpose. Gov. Parnell, anxious to justify his choice, described her as a "most estimable woman, thoroughly capable, [whose] services in the U.S. Senate will be an honor to the state." Friends seeking to secure her party nomination assured the press that she "was in great demand as a speaker before women's clubs on political questions." Delighted feminists, rejoicing over her nomination, informed reporters that "no one is so well fitted to fill her husband's vacancy as Mrs. Caraway" and predicted, "Mrs. Caraway would aid in removing inequalities against women in the law." Excited journalists added their own embellishments to the already exalted estimates. The *New York Times* reported that "her husband frequently sought her advice," the *Washington Post* noted that she "was a close adviser of Sen. Caraway on all important questions," and the *Arkansas Gazette* reported that "she will sit in the Senate chamber thoroughly familiar with its procedures and with the problems that confront that august body." In fact, the *Gazette* story continued, "Fighting Thad himself was no more shrewd and astute a politician than she." Much of this reportage, whether calculated or careless, was nonsense.[75]

Hattie Caraway was not an average housewife of the time. She had more than the ordinary amount of education and she lived amid politics and politicians all her adult life. One person who knew her well recently described her as being "witty, shrewd, with a keen political sense." Another remarked that "she was the kind of woman who really preferred living in a man's world."[76] She had not been, however, by any stretch of the imagination, a power behind Thad's throne or a political actor in her own right. Her club memberships were literary rather than political; and until July 1932, by her own admission, she had never made a speech in her life.[77]

Several months after Hattie had been serving in the Senate, a story written for the *Gazette* by a Caraway family friend (an article praised in the journal as "a wonderful writeup") provided a much more accurate and realistic account.[78] It pointed out that Hattie had rarely been seen at her husband's office and was not conspicuous as a Senate fan. It continued,

> Contrary to current assumption, Mrs. Caraway was not the counselor of her husband in political affairs. Rather she was his ready listener, his sympathetic companion, his understanding confidant. . . . Her mental endowments enabled her to grasp his problems and to give him always an appreciative ear. . . . But she never assumed the role of campaign manager. Her position was rather that of a silent partner of her husband.[79]

Nevertheless against the earliest exalted predictions of Hattie Caraway's potential, some of the later assessments stand in sharp, almost brutal, contrast: "Hattie Caraway remained for thirteen years a housewife among politicians;" "the quiet little grandmother who never won anything, lost anything, said anything or did anything. . . . thrust by the whim of the electorate into a job far beyond her capacities;" and "the first woman elected (and re-elected) to the Senate, she would be remembered for that accomplishment alone—and by some for the promise she did not keep."[80]

The journal is extremely useful in illuminating the character and explaining the behavior of an individual considerably less dazzling than some of the earliest accounts had promised, but much more impressive than the last accounts indicate. At the beginning of the journal, it is painfully apparent that Sen. Caraway is over her head. On one early occasion, not knowing how to vote, she does not vote at all, thereby creating a tie and, inadvertently, the proposed amendment's defeat. "Guess I'll have to get a system," she notes with concern. "Aye one amendment, nay, the next."[81] But she does not use this formula, learning instead to take her cues from those she trusts as sharing her basically progressive economic outlook. Frequently, however, she fixes on some witticism, or some especially vivid illustration, not because of its centrality to the debate but because it is comprehensible.

Her provincialism is repeatedly apparent in ways that are often amusing ("Hooee!! Somebody's shirt is torn"), sometimes embarrassing ("In the midst of life we are in death is certainly true these days"), occasionally distasteful ("A Miss Silverman or Stein or something Jewish pushed into my office"), and frequently touching. She is jokingly asked the color of Queen Elizabeth's wedding gown and remembers "just in time that she poor thing was never a bride."[82]

Reflecting a pattern still evident among women who take their deceased husband's seat in Congress, she is fiercely, some would say blindly, partisan.[83] Although she occasionally acknowledges the personal kindness of an individual Republican senator, she is utterly convinced of the insincerity and heartlessness of the Republican party in general and of their President Hoover in particular. By this time, of course, many Americans were speaking of Hoover in terms of total contempt: the squalid shacks of the unemployed appearing on the outskirts of every major city were called Hoovervilles, and the newspapers their inhabitants used for warmth were termed Hoover blankets. Nevertheless coming from the lips of a United States Senator, Hattie's incessant gibes and sometimes truly dreadful poems have an unpleasantly childish ring.

The only thing lower, in her view, than a Republican is a "wet" Republican. She repeatedly expresses her adamant opposition to the repeal of prohibition; and though her journal frequently indicates that she is a compassionate person, when her own brother runs afoul of the liquor laws she remarks, "If he was guilty I'm glad they caught him."[84]

She is not much more favorably disposed, although there are only two specific references, to self-proclaimed feminists. She "nixes" eulogizing Susan B. Anthony and expresses a strong distaste for former Rep. Jeanette Rankin.[85] However—and in some ways this is the journal's most interesting aspect—Sen. Caraway is acutely conscious of, and frequently resentful of, the ways in which her gender make her a second-class citizen in the Senate. In one of her first entries, a Senate employee has pointed out that Hattie has been given the same desk as that used by the first woman senator, Rebecca Felton. "I guess," the journal caustically notes, "they wanted as few of them contaminated as possible." Other clicks of feminist consciousness come when she notes that her colleagues' language excludes her and that Senate facilities do not envision a woman's presence. In her mind, the major obstacle to reelection is not that she broke a promise but that she broke with masculine tradition. When she decides to take the risk and run, she lists among her reasons, "because I really want to try out my own theory of a woman running for office."[86]

Although Sen. Caraway did eventually cosponsor the Equal Rights Amendment, and eventually made some very positive statements regarding women in politics, she never became a vocal champion of women's causes.[87] In fact, she was so rarely vocal on any subject—a most atypical characteristic of United States senators—that silence became her trademark, and she became known as "Silent Hattie," or "The Woman Who Holds Her Tongue."[88] Inasmuch as the silence of newcomers has long been one of the most hallowed folkways of the Senate, Hattie's original reticence was understandable. The pattern persisted, however, throughout her Senate career. By one count, in thirteen years she made only fifteen speeches on the Senate floor.[89]

Inevitably her silence became so obvious as to create comment, and Sen. Caraway developed a number of facile justifications for it: that she did not want to waste the taxpayers' money on paying for printing speeches in the *Congressional Record*; that Senate debate was not as important as work in committee; that "we could have much less of it [talk] and get more done and save lots of money;" and "I haven't the heart to take a minute away from the men. The poor dears love it so."[90]

Judging by the journal, there was some genuine basis for these public rationalizations. Caraway repeatedly expresses impatience with what she considers to be the grandstanding antics of her colleagues and with their tendency to belabor the obvious. "More pure bunk to the square inch today than I have seen," she notes. Even Sen. Long occasionally tries her patience with an oratorical marathon.[91] Much more significant than her impatience, however, and what becomes in many ways the journal's theme, is her acute awareness of her own visibility and vulnerability—both closely related to the fact of being female.

Decades later, it is almost impossible to comprehend fully the extreme curiosity and hostility that Hattie's presence in the Senate aroused. The curiosity is evident from the endless parade of reporters and writers noted in the journal as coming by for pictures, quotes, and interviews. The hostility is somewhat more subtle. Nothing so visibly unfriendly greeted Sen. Caraway as greeted Sen. Rebecca Felton, whose one speech caused such consternation to her colleagues that "a few buried their faces in their hands in dismay at the idea of a woman in their august midst."[92] Nevertheless it was abundantly evident that twelve years after women's nationwide enfranchisement, many people were still unconvinced of the propriety of a woman serving in the Senate.

When the State Democratic Committee was first debating her nomination, some committeemen openly and flatly stated that they were opposed to women in public office.[93] The *New York Times*, with somewhat more delicacy but clear chauvinism nonetheless, chastened Arkansas for sending Hattie Caraway to the

Senate because, "If ever there was a period in which it is essential to choose discriminatingly those who make the people's government, that period is now."[94] One article, describing the wholly masculine atmosphere of the Senate, coyly warned, "Her colleagues will have to brush up on their etiquette and make the Marble Room and other private retiring rooms more like drawing rooms," and went on to describe a few objects that "would be of interest to women: two cloisonne vases, an extravagant mirror, and a homemade silk flag."[95]

For any woman, the situation would have presented extraordinary difficulties and might well have suggested a very low profile as the safest course. For Sen. Caraway, other circumstances undoubtedly compounded the caveats against speaking out. Shy by nature, southern by background, she had been reared in a home atmosphere that emphasized women were to be ladylike, and politics was definitely not ladylike.[96] Even in adulthood, she had been deliberately schooled in silence. She told one reporter how, as the wife of a senator, she "had learned to be judiciously silent when out in public," perhaps recalling an incident when she had been outspokenly critical of a benefit singing performance by President Woodrow Wilson's daughter Margaret and been sharply rebuked by Thad at home afterward.[97] Not only was she wholly inexperienced, she was following in the footsteps of a husband whose reputation had been built on his oratorical skill and seemingly effortless eloquence.

According to recent research, the fear of seeming overly loquacious and thereby confirming a "talkative woman" stereotype is still so strong that women legislators even now feel they must speak out less, and be better prepared when they do, than their male colleagues.[98] Sen. Caraway was clearly conscious of this stereotype: "And they say women talk all the time."[99]

The constraints against speaking, then, were numerous and powerful from the beginning. The journal also records a number of negative reinforcements, experiences in which Sen. Caraway learned (and apparently never forgot) that anything she said might come back to haunt her. An encounter with a reporter "who made me out a communist" leaves her totally distraught and vowing not to give any more interviews. Worried after a conversation with Sen. Joseph T. Robinson, she wonders, "Guess I said too much or too little. Never know." Frequently she tries to disguise her unease with awkward attempts at humor but learns that this too can be dangerous: "How awful that men always think evilly or unkindly. I did say a fool thing to Bankhead—but it was innocently done, and I'm not going to worry. I'll quit talking to them all."[100]

For Sen. Caraway, silence was more than a natural tendency, reinforced by social sanctions and compounded by inexperience. It was a deliberately self-imposed shield against the ever-present possibilities of misunderstanding, criticism, and ridicule. The record of her reticence has been somewhat exaggerated. In her whirlwind campaign with Sen. Long, for example, although her first efforts at public speaking were, by her own admission, disastrous, she seems to have quickly learned the knack of playing a crowd with brief but well-chosen words.[101] A scrapbook of newspaper clippings records many later instances when she made brief remarks to political gatherings, club meetings, and college commencements.[102] In fact, she made a speech seconding President Roosevelt's renomination at the Democratic National Convention in 1936. She never, however, spoke more than was necessary—a silence that the journal makes more understandable.

Modern readers may wish that Sen. Caraway had been more outspoken or that she had used her sturdy sense of social justice to become a more forceful legislative leader. Feminists in particular might well wish that her obvious consciousness of the subordinate status of her sex had been forged into more productive purposes. Such did not happen, of course; and even to wish that it might is to impose our desires and values upon her retrospectively. What did happen is that a determined woman struggled through a maze of discouraging circumstances to achieve—not just be assigned—her own seat in the Senate, and performed the functions of that office with sufficient capability to survive.

After she had confounded the politicians and political prophets by winning reelection in 1932, the citizens of Jonesboro (many of whom had been the last to jump on her bandwagon) held a city-wide homecoming in her honor.[103] One of her deceased husband's law partners presented her to the crowd by noting that "it required more moral courage and more physical courage for

Mrs. Caraway to enter this campaign than was required of any general who ever led an army into battle.[104] The hyperbole is a bit thick for our contemporary tastes. However, considering the abundant evidence from recent research indicating that the actual decision to run for office represents a major, perhaps the major, obstacle to the presence of more women in elective office, Sen. Caraway's decision is still impressive by today's standards.[105]

The journal in many ways is a record of personal growth, of one woman's development from a timid and self-deprecating widow, trying to make up "what passes for my mind," to a spunky and self-confident politician resentful that she is still, years later, being treated as a fluke.[106] Some of her remarks sound silly and shallow to our long-emancipated ears. On balance, however, she deserves from us more compassion than condescension and more respect for what she did achieve than regret for what she did not.

NOTES

1. For discussion of the "widow's succession" route to Congress and some of the false impressions traditionally surrounding it, see Diane Kincaid, "Over His Dead Body: A Positive Perspective on Widows in the U.S. Congress," *Western Political Quarterly* (March 1978): 96-104.

2. This expression is quoted by William R. Kennan, "Senator Hattie Caraway: A Study in Rhetorical Efficacy" (Master's thesis, University of Arkansas, 1976), p. 38, and Betty M. Sneed, "Hattie Wyatt Caraway: United States Senator, 1931-1945" (Master's thesis, University of Arkansas, 1975), p. 6, and seems to be derived from a 1950 interview with E. J. Bodman, *Arkansas Gazette*, December 24, 1950, recalling events that occurred eighteen years previously. Inasmuch as Sen. Thad Caraway was an original supporter of the Equal Rights Amendment, and a condolence telegram from Alice Paul to Hattie Caraway (in the Thaddeus Caraway Scrapbook) states, "The National Women's Party owes a great debt to Sen. Caraway and feels that the whole women's movement has lost one of its best friends," his opposition to women in politics seems dubious.

3. Statement by A. C. Grigson, *Arkansas Gazette*, March 15, 1978.

4. Journal, January 25, 1934.

5. The most comprehensive study to date of the life of Hattie Caraway is Sneed, "Hattie Wyatt Caraway." A few additional details are provided in Hope Chamberlin, *A Minority of Members* (New York: Praeger

Publishers, 1973), pp. 89-99; Annabelle Paxton, *Women in Congress* (Richmond, Va.: Dietz Press, 1945), pp. 17-28; and Louise M. Young, "Hattie Ophelia Wyatt Caraway," in *Notable American Women, 1607-1950*, ed. Edward T. James (Cambridge: Belknap Press of Harvard University Press, 1971), pp. 284-286.

6. According to E. J. Bodman, a Little Rock banker, Thad Caraway mentioned to Bodman in the fall of 1931 that he needed surgery but could not afford it because his property in both Washington and Jonesboro was heavily mortgaged and he had borrowed to the limit on his life insurance. Bodman arranged with the Catholic bishop in Little Rock, who was grateful for Thad's courage in the Ku Klux Klan days, for free treatment at St. Vincent's Hospital. Because of these events, when Thad died Bodman knew how dismal Hattie's financial situation as a widow would be. My interviews in Jonesboro confirmed that the Caraways' financial situation was indeed bleak, but the reasons offered varied from "Thad was too honest to use that office to make money" to "He spent it on some wild living." Bodman interview in *Arkansas Gazette*, December 24, 1950.

7. This being prior to passage of the Twentieth, or "Lame Duck," Amendment to the United States Constitution, congressmen were elected in November of even-numbered years and served until the term of a new Congress began in March two and one-half years later. Thad Caraway's term, therefore, would have expired in March 1933.

8. Harry Lee Williams, *Forty Years Behind The Scenes in Arkansas Politics* (Little Rock: Parkin Printing & Stationery Co., 1949), p. 26.

9. *Arkansas Gazette*, November 28, 1931.

10. Ibid., December 30, 1931.

11. Ibid., December 2, 1931.

12. Ibid., January 13, 1932.

13. *Memphis Commercial Appeal*, May 10, 1932; *Jonesboro Sun*, May 10, 1932.

14. Further depressing the outlook for Sen. Caraway, and calming the opposition, were two additional factors: her own Craighead County had by this time been well organized by the Democratic county chairman, Charles Frierson, for O. L. Bodenhamer; and the campaign manager she eventually announced was a young man, Marshall Purvis of Hot Springs, with virtually no political connections or experience.

15. A prediction quoted by Hermann B. Deutsch, "Hattie and Huey," *Saturday Evening Post*, October 15, 1932, p. 7.

16. The most extensive accounts of this colorful campaign appear in ibid., pp. 6-7, 88-90, 92, and in the *Arkansas Gazette* campaign coverage

of August 1-9, 1932. Some additional details are provided in Stuart Towns, "A Louisiana Medicine Show: The Kingfish Elects an Arkansas Senator" *Arkansas Historical Quarterly* (Summer 1966): 117-127; and T. Harry Williams, *Huey Long* (New York: Alfred A. Knopf, 1969), pp. 583-618.

17. Quoted in Williams, *Huey Long*, p. 588; *Arkansas Gazette*, August 4, 1932; Deutsch, "Hattie and Huey," p. 92.

18. *Arkansas Gazette*, August 2, 1932.

19. At this time, a majority was not required to win the nomination; hence no runoff was required. In November 1932, Republican candidate John White polled 21,558 votes to Sen. Caraway's 187,999.

20. Young, "Hattie Caraway," p. 286.

21. Interviews with family members assured me that it is highly unlikely the journal was kept at other times and that, if it had been, nothing more than what is printed here has been preserved.

22. *Journal*, February 11, 1932.

23. Ibid., March 11, 1932.

24. Ibid., March 28, 1934.

25. See for example, John D. Hicks, *Republican Ascendancy, 1921-1933* (New York: Harper and Row, 1963), pp. 215-280; Arthur M. Schlesinger, Jr., *The Crisis of the Old Order, 1919-33* (Boston: Houghton Mifflin, 1956), pp. 155-269; David A. Shannon, *Between the Wars: America, 1919-1941* (Boston: Houghton Mifflin, 1965), pp. 107-146; and Gene Smith, *The Shattered Dream* (New York: William Morrow, 1970), pp. 55-82.

26. *Arkansas Gazette*, December 24, 1950.

27. Mary Jane Moffat and Charlotte Painter, *Revelations: Diaries of Women* (New York: Random House, 1975), pp. 1-10.

28. Journal, June 9, 1932.

29. Ibid., March 17, May 9, 1932.

30. Ibid., May 5, 1932.

31. Ibid., March 22, 1932.

32. Ibid., May 3, February 5, 1932.

33. Ibid., March 16, 1932.

34. Ibid., February 29, 1932.

35. Kincaid, "Over His Dead Body," p. 96.

36. Quoted by Chamberlin, *Minority of Members*, p. 91, as a phrase often used in describing Hattie Caraway.

37. For example, see stories in *Arkansas Gazette*, November 10, 11, 14, 1931; *New York Times*, November 15, 1931; and *Washington Post*, November 10, 1931.

38. *Arkansas Gazette*, December 2, 1931.

39. Ibid., November 10, 1931; *Jonesboro Daily Tribune*, November 10, 1931.

40. This statement is based on an extensive search of all the major Arkansas newspapers of this period and on an exhaustive tracking down of all those disclaimers attributed to Hattie Caraway. Invariably the statements came instead from someone claiming to be speaking in her behalf.

41. The particular impediments that southern culture has imposed against political activity by women have been documented by Anne Firor Scott, *The Southern Lady: From Pedestal to Politics, 1830-1930* (Chicago: University of Chicago Press, 1970).

42. Telephone interview with Anne Hawthorne Ramey, Jonesboro, Arkansas, June 23, 1978.

43. Personal interview with Bill Penix, Jonesboro, Arkansas, June 22, 1978, who recalled Harvey Parnell telling his father, Roy Penix (once a law partner of Thad Caraway's), that Hattie personally promised she would not run.

44. Williams, *Forty Years*, p. 28. Williams' statement that Parnell had intended to announce but refrained from doing so after Hattie entered the race, and died a few years later a "crestfallen, broken-hearted man," ignores the fact that Parnell did announce for the Senate early in 1932 but later backed out of politics completely when a Highway Department audit and bond defaults threatened his viability as a candidate for anything.

45. Sneed, "Hattie Wyatt Caraway," p. 5, quotes a "letter from a friend of Sen. Caraway who does not wish his name mentioned" that assurances came directly from Hattie. Two people I interviewed, one in Jonesboro and one in Washington, D.C., expressed the same opinion but asked that they not be quoted. John Wells, "Origin of the Hatch Act," *Little Rock Weekly News Review*, June 17, 1978, p. 4, says Hattie herself promised not to run but that this statement could have been interpreted only as a promise not to run against Parnell, who was forced to withdraw for reasons unrelated to her announced candidacy.

46. This affidavit, in the possession of John Wells, a Little Rock publisher, is extremely interesting but not altogether persuasive. The statement, sworn to before a notary public on October 16, 1937, states that its author (an organizer of the Arkansas Women's Democratic Club), was told by Gov. Parnell that Hattie, through one of her sons, had promised not to seek another term and that in this son's presence, a wealthy friend of the Caraways and of Parnell promised a $10,000 campaign contribution to Parnell's 1932 Senate race if Parnell would give the interim appointment to and secure the party's nomination for Hattie. The affidavit's author does not claim to have been present when this offer was made and accepted, and the son in question, although remembering a long

encounter with and much pressure from the financial backer in question, insists there was no such meeting involving himself, the financier, and Parnell.

47. Paul Caraway, for example, recalls a steady stream of "interested parties" pressing for such a commitment from both himself and his brother Forrest, both of whom were politically inexperienced. When the two brothers finally got together and realized they were being "whip-sawed," they refused to discuss the matter further with outsiders and insisted that only their mother could speak for herself. Personal interview, Washington, D.C., July 9, 1978.

48. See, for example, E. J. Bodman interview, *Arkansas Gazette*, December 24, 1950. Some people I interviewed in Jonesboro were as convinced as Bodman that Hattie never explicitly promised not to run: Joe Barrett, a law partner of Thad, because "I would have known if such a promise were made" and because "it would have been totally out of character for Mrs. Caraway to break a promise"; Joe Martin, who became Hattie's area campaign manager and later her home office aide, because she was too deliberate in her decision making to have been willing to commit herself so quickly to such a major future commitment. Personal interviews, June 23, 1978.

49. Interview, July 9, 1978.

50. Telephone interview, Washington, D.C., July 10, 1978, with a long-time observer of and participant in Arkansas politics, who preferred not to be quoted.

51. Journal, February 24, 1932.

52. See, for example, ibid., March 16, 24, 25, April 21, 29, 30, 1932.

53. Ibid., February 19, 29, April 12, 1932.

54. *Arkansas Gazette*, December 24, 1950.

55. Journal, May 16, 1932.

56. Ibid., May 11, 16, 1932.

57. Sharpe Dunaway, quoted in William Curtis Mears, "L. S. (Sharpe) Dunaway," *Arkansas Historical Quarterly* (1954): 81, and Towns, "A Louisiana Medicine Show," p. 127, both flatly state that Long won the election for her. Williams, *Huey Long*, pp. 592-593, suggests that the support of Arkansas' depression-pinched farmers, aware that Thad Caraway had been their vocal champion and that Hattie Caraway was their strong supporter, would have put her "around the midpoint or even above it in the final standing of the candidates. What Huey had done . . . was to arouse into a full fury this resentment vaguely felt by the farmers, to weld it, really, into a genuine class protest."

58. *Arkansas Gazette*, August 11, 1932.

59. Senator Tom Connally of Texas expressed this opinion in *My Name Is Tom Connally* (New York: Thomas Y. Crowell, 1954), p. 167, as did Marshall Purvis, Hattie's 1932 statewide campaign manager, in an interview after Long's death, *Arkansas Democrat*, September 11, 1932.

60. According to the journal, Hattie decides to run on May 9, 1932; Long makes his offer of assistance on May 21, 1932.

61. These explanations are offered by Thomas Martin, *Dynasty: The Longs of Louisiana* (New York: G. P. Putnam's, 1960), pp. 108-109; Towns, "Louisiana Medicine Show," pp. 121-122; Williams, *Huey Long*, p. 584, 586-587.

62. Burton K. Wheeler, *Yankee from the West* (Garden City, N.Y.: Doubleday, 1962), pp. 280-281.

63. Williams, *Huey Long*, p. 587.

64. Journal, December 17, 1931.

65. Ibid., February 3, 25, 1932.

66. Ibid., March 14, 21, 1932.

67. Long characteristically wore "pongee suits with orchid-colored shirts, striped straw hats, watermelon-pink ties, and brown and white sport shoes." William E. Leuchtenburg, *Franklin D. Roosevelt and the New Deal, 1932-1940* (New York: Harper and Row, 1963), p. 97. Deutsch, "Hattie and Huey," p. 92; journal, May 12, 1932.

68. Ibid., May 16, 30, 1932.

69. Ibid., May 5, 21, 1932.

70. Interview with Marshall Purvis, *Arkansas Democrat*, September 11, 1935; interview with Hattie Caraway, *Arkansas Gazette*, September 11, 1932; George Creel, "The Woman Who Holds Her Tongue," *Collier's*, September 18, 1937, p. 22; Wheeler, *Yankee from the West*, p. 281.

71. Long told *Arkansas Gazette* reporters that he and Robinson "would settle their differences in the Senate" (August 2, 1932) and that he would "refrain from discussing his [Robinson's] record except when it is necessary to call attention to it in a general way in presenting Mrs. Caraway's record" (August 4, 1932).

72. Travis Martin Adams, "The Arkansas Congressional Delegation During the New Deal, 1933-36" (Master's thesis, Vanderbilt University, 1962), pp. 18-22, 104-105, 214, and Sneed, "Hattie Caraway," pp. 44-45.

73. *Literary Digest*, September 4, 1937; *Arkansas Gazette*, March 25, 1935. That Hattie was not completely compliant with Long's wishes is further suggested by Marshall Purvis' claim (*Arkansas Democrat*, September 11, 1935) that Long was bitterly disappointed in Hattie's failure to "stand shoulder to shoulder with him."

74. *Arkansas Gazette*, November 10, 1931; *New York Times*, November

15, 1931; *Washington Post*, November 10, 1931.

75. *Arkansas Gazette*, November 10, 14, 1931; *Washington Post*, November 13, 1931; *New York Times*, November 15, 1931.

76. Telephone interview with Anne Hawthorne Ramey, Jonesboro, Arkansas, June 23, 1978; personal interview with Della (Mrs. Paul) Caraway, Washington, D.C., July 9, 1978.

77. *Arkansas Gazette*, July 20, 1932.

78. Journal, March 1, 1932.

79. "Junior Senator from Arkansas," *Arkansas Gazette Magazine*, February 28, 1932, p. 5 (probably written by Charlotte Frierson). See journal, March 1, 1932, n. 2.

80. Kennan, "Senator Hattie Caraway," p. 54. Allen Drury, *A Senate Journal, 1943-1945* (New York: Da Capo Press, 1972), pp. 224-225. Chamberlin, *Minority of Members*, p. 99.

81. Journal, January 9, 1932.

82. Ibid., December 15, 1931, February 3, 8, 16, 1932.

83. Kathleen A. Frankovic, "Sex and Voting in the U.S. House of Representatives: 1961-1975," *American Politics Quarterly* (July 1977): 324, finds higher party loyalty among the "widows," both Democratic and Republican, than among congresswomen generally and suggests that possibly "party cues are necessary for those without prior political experience, particularly for those women who are in Congress, at least originally, solely because of their relationship to another member of the House."

84. Journal, February 18, 1932.

85. Ibid., February 10, May 2, 1932.

86. Ibid., December 15, 1931, January 4, February 16, May 9, 13, 1932.

87. See, for example, statements by Hattie in *Coronet*, June 1941, and January 1942, and in *The Ideal Woman*, January 1942. These items, neither titled nor paginated, are in Hattie Caraway Scrapbook, Special Collections, University of Arkansas. Also see Hattie Caraway quotes in *Washington Evening Star*, April 7, 1936, *Washington Post*, November 29, 1940, and *New York Times*, February 23, 1943.

88. "Silent Hattie" cited by Kennan, "Senator Hattie Caraway," p. 7; Creel, "Woman Who Holds Her Tongue."

89. "Last of the First," *Time*, August 7, 1944, p. 19.

90. *Arkansas Gazette*, August 2, 1932, June 29, 1944; *Northwest Arkansas Times*, June 29, 1944; Creel, "Woman Who Holds Her Tongue," p. 55.

91. Journal, January 21, 1932. Also see ibid., February 3, 5, 8, April 5, 1932.

92. *Arkansas Gazette*, February 2, 1943.

93. Ibid., December 2, 1931.

94. *New York Times* editorial, November 20, 1931.

95. "The Senate and Women," *Pathfinder* (1931), in Hattie Caraway Scrapbook.

96. Telephone interview with Susan Renfro, a niece of Hattie Caraway, who described the Wyatt family as having very traditional views regarding the appropriate role of women. Washington, D.C., July 10, 1978.

97. *New York Times*, December 8, 1931. An incident recalled by Paul Caraway, personal interview, July 9, 1978.

98. *Women State Legislators: Report from a Conference* (New Brunswick, N.J.: Eagleton Institute, Center for the Study of Women in Politics, May 1973), p. 8.

99. Journal, December 22, 1931.

100. Ibid., February 25, 29, March 30, 1932.

101. Deutsch, "Hattie and Huey," pp. 89-90.

102. Hattie Caraway Scrapbook.

103. According to several people I interviewed in Jonesboro, when Hattie first announced she was going to seek reelection, the political establishment in Jonesboro was already committed to O. L. Bodenhamer. Joe Martin, at that time a newcomer to politics, was pressed into making the necessary local logistical arrangements for Hattie's appearance with Huey Long by his friend and former roommate, Marshall Purvis.

104. Judge J. F. Gautney, quoted in *Arkansas Gazette*, August 17, 1932. The homecoming almost turned into disaster when hungry bystanders became so aroused by the odor of barbecuing hams that they stormed the premises and had to be routed by the local fire department. Personal interview with Bill Penix, June 23, 1978.

105. That the actual decision to compete is a paramount obstacle to women seeking elective office has been suggested by and substantiated in Marcia Lee, "Toward Understanding Why Few Women Hold Public Office," in *A Portrait of Marginality: The Political Behavior of the American Woman*, ed. Marianne Githins and Jewel L. Prestage (New York: David McKay, 1977), pp. 118-138; A. Karnig and O. Walter, "Elections of Women to City Councils," *Social Science Quarterly* (March 1976): 605-613; and Jeane J. Kirkpatrick, *Political Woman* (New York: Basic Books, 1974), pp. 59-84.

106. *Journal*, December 22, 1931, March 28, 1934.

II
JOURNAL

ABOUT THE ANNOTATION

Hattie Caraway's journal is reproduced here exactly as she wrote it except that the dating style has been made uniform. Her occasional misspellings of names and incorrect identifications of individuals are clarified, where necessary, in footnotes. Since most of the entries were written while she sat on the Senate floor, headnotes have been used to explain the Senate business in process. Footnotes are used for additional identifications, clarifications, and sources. Some individuals appear so frequently that, after the first extensive identification, they will not be repeatedly identified. Some individuals mentioned in the journal eluded all efforts at identification and are simply noted as "not identified."

DECEMBER 14, 1931

*The first entry records an incident during a speech by Sen.
Clarence C. Dill (D-Wash.) advocating an international mone-
tary conference to establish silver as a basis for world exchange: Charles Curtis (R-Kan.), vice-president of the United
States and therefore president of the Senate, intends to recognize Sen. Hiram W. Johnson (R-Cal.), but Sen. Samuel M.
Shortridge (R-Cal.) responds.*

A funny thing today. The two Sen.s from California were both
asking for recognition. The V.P. looked at the Senior Sen. and
recognized the Gentleman from Cal. and both gave a surprised
grin when the tall Cedar of Lebanon the Jr. Sen. responded. Guess
such things happen often but it was amusing to me. Sen. Dill is
making a Speech. I think he must use a blackening for his mustache.

Sen. Harris told me some Forestry Com. had bought 190000
acres of land in N.W. Ark. — and some more in the Ozarks.[1]

1. Sen. William J. Harris (D-Ga.) referring to a proposed addition to the Ozark
National Forest.

DECEMBER 15, 1931

*While the Senate debates first a bill to coordinate federal
wildlife preservation programs and then President Hoover's
proposed moratorium on war-engendered debts owed to the
United States by foreign governments, Sen. Caraway presages
what become some major themes: the manners and dress of
her colleagues, her impatience with their long-windedness,
her fiercely partisan anti-Hooverism, her distrust of the press,
and her acute awareness that her sex makes her an outsider in
the Senate.*

Sen Lewis[1] is dressed in a tan shirt with green stripes, green tie low cut vest of creame—looks like linen—Beige Spats. His shirt sleeves are very long cuff buttons of enamel, black ground with red flowers. Mr. Dill's[2] mustache seems to be making him responsible for all legislation. At least he is moved to question every angle of every bill up so far.

Hiram Johnson[3] arises to compliment all and sundry. Very fiery and far too long.

Sen. Simmons[4] looks so wrinkled and worn both as to his physical condition and dress it is pitiful to see him. Mr. Gerry[5] looks fine—a little more gray in his hair—and a rather gray cast to his complexion. He is nice too—and his old friends seem really pleased to see him. Sen. Shipstead[6] not a charming speaker. Guess there will be no vote on Moses today.[7] Sen. Black[8] waxed eloquent on the subject of the 7 million unemployed, and lectured the Senate on taking any other vote on Pres. Pro tem. Drew several picture profiles of Senators sitting in front of me.[9]

The 1st of the Senate Luncheons. Mrs. Blaine and Mrs. Waterman[10] called on me at the office. Mr. Halsey[11] has just told me that I have the same desk as the one used by Mrs. Felton.[12] I guess they wanted as few of them contaminated as possible. There is the vote. I've yelled Pittman once again.[13] A Miss Silverman or Stein or something Jewish pushed into my office. I was terribly indignant. She got no interview, but no telling what she may write. Sen. Simmons came in like a ghost and got some notice. How can they come back? It seems to me the chagrin would prevent. Tom Heflin parades around to the especial disgust of Bankhead.[14] I hope to remember to take note of the rotation in the color schemes of the apparel of the Jr. Sen. from Ill. Mr. Lewis.

They're still discussing *wild life* and I'm getting very hungry. Think I shall introduce a bill for a regular luncheon hour. All Senators to be fired if they do not eat in that hour.

Sen. McKellar[15] at 1:55 P.M. is reeling off figures in millions and millions. War debts etc. His hair is beautifully brushed and a silk handkerchief, white dots on a blue ground, peeps rather more than demurely from his pocket. Dave Reed[16] spoke my sentiments on cancellation of war debts. Smoot[17] and Glass[18] locked horns on the State Dept. approving private loans to foreign countries. I think Glass is right-naturally. Dad thought Smoot was nearly always wrong naturally.[19]

1. Sen. J. Hamilton Lewis (D-Ill.) had served in the Senate from 1913 to 1919, ran unsuccessfully for Illinois governor in 1920, and was again elected to the Senate in 1930. Noted for his colorful dress, "Jim Ham" Lewis sits one seat away from Sen. Caraway on the last row, where she can clearly view his ever-changing costume.

2. Sen. Clarence C. Dill (D-Wash.).

3. Sen. Hiram W. Johnson (R-Cal.).

4. Former Sen. Furnifold M. Simmons (D-N.C.), who retired March 4, 1931, at age seventy-seven, after thirty years continuous service in the Senate.

5. Former Sen. Peter G. Gerry (D-R.I.).

6. Sen. Henrik Shipstead (Farmer-Labor-Minn.).

7. Sen. George H. Moses (R-N.H.), president pro tempore of the Senate, infuriated the Senate's bloc of progressive Republicans by referring to them in a speech to a gathering of New England manufacturers on November 7, 1929, as "Sons of the Wild Jackass." In revenge, they refused to support his bid for reelection as president pro tempore.

8. Sen. Hugo L. Black (D-Ala.).

9. Sen. Caraway frequently sketched portraits and caricatures of her colleagues while seated on the floor. None can now be located.

10. Wives of Sen. John J. Blaine (R-Wisc.) and Sen. Charles W. Waterman (R-Colo.).

11. Edwin A. Halsey, secretary to the minority.

12. Rebecca Latimer Felton was given an interim appointment to the United States Senate by Georgia's governor on October 3, 1922, to fill a vacancy created by Sen. Thomas Watson's death. Gov. Hardwick intended the appointment as an act of pure tokenism, to appease the recently enfranchised women whose suffrage he had opposed, but eighty-seven-year-old Felton instigated a nationwide barrage of letters to President Harding for a special congressional session to swear her in before her brief term expired. A special session did become necessary, she was duly sworn, and served in the Senate from November 21 to November 22, 1922.

13. In the vote for president pro tempore, Sen. Caraway consistently voted with the Democrats for Sen. Key Pittman (D-Nev.).

14. Former Senator Thomas J. Heflin (D-Ala.) was defeated by Sen. John H. Bankhead in 1930, but Heflin has challenged the legality of Bankhead's election (see journal entry for April 21, 1932), hence his lingering presence in the Senate.

15. Sen. Kenneth McKellar (D-Tenn.).

16. Sen. David A. Reed (R-Pa.).

17. Sen. Reed Smoot (R-Utah).

18. Sen. Carter Glass (D-Va.).

19. "Dad" is the late Sen. Thaddeus H. Caraway, whose partisanship "naturally" led to his support for Democrat Glass and disagreement with Republican Smoot.

DECEMBER 16, 1931

*Senate debate continues on S. 263, to ensure adequate sup-
plies of wildlife, and another inconclusive vote is taken to fill
the office of president pro tempore.*

Got in just after prayer. Ans. Quorum all. Rising vote on calling
up a bill for protection of wild life.

Mr. Moses gave me a room in capitol—No. 42—at request of
Mr. Halsey.[1]

Sen. Logan[2] Ky—has that round beer barrel figure of the typi-
cal Ky. cononel. And the rather high soprano which always sur-
prises one when it issues from a man of that size. He does seem
nice though. He has one of the heaviest suits of hair in the Senate
and has yet to disprove the old saying that hair and brains do not
go together.

Another vote for Pres. Pro-tem at 1:15 P.M. making eighteen in
all. Mr. Hebert[3] got some votes today.

Jim Ham went to a verbal duel with the press for saying I was
"plain Mrs. Caraway"—He wore same shirt—spats and vest—but
a black tie embroidered in green.

1. Sen. Caraway was offered her late husband's office but instructed Edwin
Halsey, minority secretary, to request the office assignment from president pro
tempore George Moses that would be accorded any newcomer.
2. Sen. Marvel Mills Logan (D-Ky.).
3. Sen. Felix Hebert (R-R.I.).

DECEMBER 17, 1931

*The Senate transacts no official business this day but hears
some spirited oratory, primarily from Sen. Joseph T. Robinson
(D-Ark.) and Sen. Pat Harrison (D-Miss.), furiously responding
to charges levied against congressional Democrats at a meeting that week of the Republican National Committee. Robinson also tangles with Sen. William E. Borah (R-Idaho), who
opposes a lengthy Senate recess.*

Hattie Caraway seated at her Senate desk, December 1931. New York Times Pictures.

Have just learned that Huey Long[1] is to have seat immediately to my left. I'm wondering if he won't have some trouble taking his seat. I'm also wondering who will escort him to take the oath. He had asked Dad to do that. He will bring color and quite a display of fireworks I imagine.

Sen. Lewis has on a wing collar and black bow tie. Same spats and vests. I haven't got the color of his shirt. Am sure he has changed though.

Our knight of the red carnation[2] is with us.

Sol Bloom[3] talked sense today. Of course men and women acquire life, intellect and character in just same way as men. With training they can be just as good politicians, etc.

Joe[4] a political speech. Pat one of facetious ones on the statement that the Com. must sell Mr. Hoover.[5] This country has been paying for him thru the nose for some years — so for heavens sake sell him out of the country. Mr. Borah suggests only 5 days recess for Christmas holidays. Joe made a speech very fiery. Sen. Lewis shirt today is an Alice blue stripe effect with black butterfly ties. Mr. Thompson came to see me. N.O. Item. Genevieve Clarkes husband.[6]

---

1. After a meteoric and bitterly controversial rise through the offices of railroad commissioner, public service commissioner, and governor, Huey P. Long (D-La.) had been elected to the Senate in November 1930 but retained his governorship to ensure it would not be filled by an unfriendly lieutenant governor.

2. Sen. Samuel M. Shortridge (R-Cal.) always wore a carnation in his buttonhole.

3. Rep. Sol. Bloom (D-N.Y.).

4. "Joe" is Sen. Joseph T. Robinson, Arkansas' other senator, who had served briefly in the United States House of Representatives and as Arkansas governor before being elected by the state legislature to the United States Senate in 1913. He was elected minority leader by his colleagues in 1922 and had been Al Smith's vice-presidential running-mate on the Democratic ticket in 1928.

5. Sen. Pat Harrison, noting the charge given to the Republican National Committee to "sell" President Hoover to the country, states, "Short selling has become so prevalent under the Hoover administration that my friend the chairman of the Republican National Committee has adopted the plan of selling Hoover short, certainly not long." Quotations from Senate debate are taken from the *Congressional Record* of that date unless otherwise identified.

6. H. O. Thompson and Delbert Clark from the United Press.

DECEMBER 18, 1931

Sen. Clarence C. Dill (D-Wash.) advocates silver as a basis for world exchange, and Sen. Kenneth McKellar (D-Tenn.) proposes an investigation of air and sea mail contracts. Weightier subjects — unemployment, faltering world markets, loans to drought-stricken farmers, investigation of the railroads — are also discussed but provoke no comment from Sen. Caraway, who is obviously exhausted.

Sen. Dill has the floor again mustache and all. Mrs. Abbott[1] came over with me. Got a box of stationery for her. 2:10. Came up in front elevator. Met Mrs. Bingham.[2] She did not present her friend. Leslie Biffle paid me 47.95 for Paul & Forrest — expenses.[3] McKellar presenting bills etc. Sen. Kendrick gave me with compliments of the com. Dad's book which held his bills.[4] Had clam chowder with Auntie,[5] Garrett[6] & Pearl[7] at Senate Office Cafe. Went downtown. Never so tired in my life.

1. Mrs. Moselle (Mosie) Abbott, Sen. Caraway's sister, then employed at the Library of Congress.

2. Wife of Sen. Hiram Bingham (R-Conn.).

3. On December 8, the Senate passed a resolution authorizing payment of certain expenses in connection with Sen. Thaddeus Caraway's funeral. Leslie Biffle, assistant secretary to the minority, probably was transmitting some of these funds. Paul and Forrest, Sen. Caraway's two older sons, were at this time both army lieutenants serving, respectively, at Army Headquarters in Washington, D.C., and at Fort Washington, Maryland.

4. Sen. John B. Kendrick (D-Wyo.) served with Thad Caraway on the Senate Agriculture and Forestry Committee.

5. "Auntie" is Sen. Caraway's usual way of referring to her sister, Mrs. Abbott.

6. Garrett Whiteside, originally from Nashville, Ark., had begun serving as a congressional secretary to Arkansas Rep. Ben Cravens in 1907, continued with Rep. Otis Wingo, then with Sen. Thaddeus Caraway, and remained Sen. Hattie Caraway's chief aide throughout her career.

7. Mrs. Garrett Whiteside.

DECEMBER 19, 1931

Sen. Caraway was given her deceased husband's seat on the Senate Agriculture and Forestry Committee and here reports

*on her first official attendance, including rather unflattering
assessments of James C. Stone, vice-chairman of the Federal
Farm Board, Sen. Charles L. McNary (R-Ore.), and Sen. John G.
Townsend (R-Del.). On the Senate floor, Sen. William H. King
(D-Utah) reluctantly consents to passage of a private claims
bill sponsored by Sen. Alben W. Barkley (D-Ky.). The Republican insurgents have now switched their president pro tempore
votes to Sen. Arthur H. Vandenberg (R-Mich.), but there is still
no majority.*

First meeting with Agricultural Committee. At 10:20 today.
Interesting. Perhaps seem futile—but some good may come out
of it. Mr. Stone of the Farm Board was present. He was pretty self
assured. Didn't appeal to me as being a sympathetic personality.
Nor of great intellectual ability. Smooth and hard is the way I'd
sum him up. Sen. McNary appears much older in close view. A
great deal of force and decision. The subject and object of the
meeting of the Com. was appropriation of 20 to 50 millions bushels
of wheat for the unemployed. Either by being on strike or really
unable to get work.[1]

Sen. Townsend is tall and large and bulbous eyed—and a very
poor reader. Sen. King threatened to object to a unanimous consent Bill of Sen. Barklay but did not excusing himself with the
prophecy we would live to rue it.

Another vote on Pres. Pro-tem. No election.

Early adjournment.

1. Farm income by this time was less than half what it had been in 1929, and the
Agriculture Committee meets almost constantly to consider proposals for dealing
with these disastrous conditions. The situation was enormously complicated by
the failure of farm leaders to agree on what governmental actions should be taken,
by the knowledge that President Hoover would veto any measure requiring more
than minimal governmental intervention, and by the tremendous suspicion farmers
felt for any governmental program after the total failure of the Federal Farm
Board. The board was established in June 1929 and appropriated $500 million with
which to stabilize prices through timely purchases of excess commodities. The
system began operating just as the stock market broke, and an agency designed
to deal with small temporary surpluses could not cope with a totally depressed
market. For a brief period, the board turned its efforts toward encouraging limited

production, but with no enforcement authority this too was futile. Eventually its holdings of wheat and cotton were processed and distributed to the needy through the Red Cross.

DECEMBER 21, 1931

The Senate is debating H. J. Res. 147 embodying President Hoover's proposed moratorium on the repayment of foreign war debts. Sen. Hiram Johnson (R-Cal.), apparently miffed by his exclusion from a White House breakfast, discusses the proposal critically, and Sen. George W. Norris (R-Neb.) and Sen. Robert B. Howell (R-Neb.) argue at length against it. Sen. Caraway responds with a poem to the suggestion that the Senate stay continuously in session until the matter is resolved. Sen. Smith W. Brookhart (R-Iowa) makes a speech criticizing the Farm Board's failure to promote a cooperative system of agricultural production.

Went to see Mrs. Nicholson. The Gen. died yesterday at 4:00 P.M.[1] Missed committee meeting. Hot discussion of adjournment. Sen. Johnson a slap because he wasn't invited to White House breakfast. (Sen. Lewis a symphony in brown today, with a grey vest and spats. I really like the reddish brown, with his shade hair and whiskers. His color scheme extends to his handkerchief which has narrow brown hem and brown stripe border.) "Moratorium has been granted unconstitutionally and illegally, but it is an accomplished fact."[2] Sen. Norris. We must go without food — we must go without sleep —

That the President's word he may be able to keep.

The Constitution and laws may all go to pot.
But what of our people? They may all rot.

We aren't humanitarian. We are only yes men.
And get up or down when Hoover says when.

If he were a man whose ideas were great.
Or wise, or unselfish. There'd not be the hate

That is felt for him now and I hope will extend
To the time when our voters will his term bring to end.

Sen. Brookhart talking on economic conditions in this country and Russia. Farm Board got some attention.

Sen. Howell keeps talking about four thousand two hundred and thirty one millions — a new way to read numbers.[3] Saw Mrs. Stanley[4] today in Senate Office Bldg. 3:15 P.M. and Sen. Howell still states and restates his position — and opposition. Had a talk with the Vice President[5] — my first. He is rather nice. Am afraid I was interviewed by World Telegram Representative. When I was all set to stay at least half the night the Senate recessed at about 5:10 until 11 A.M. Tuesday.

1. Brig. Gen. William J. ("Slicker Bill") Nicholson was a close friend of the Caraways. He had risen through the ranks of the cavalry, serving for a while as commander of the Seventh Cavalry, Gen. Custer's old regiment, and had been awarded the Distinguished Service Cross for exceptional gallantry in World War I. His wife, Harriett, is a frequent visitor.

2. Sen. Norris states, "The moratorium has been granted — unconstitutionally and illegally, but granted nevertheless; and whether we put our stamp of approval on it today or tomorrow or six weeks from now is, as I look at it, quite immaterial."

3. France owes a $4,231,000 war debt to the United States.

4. Probably Mrs. William O. Stanley of Little Rock, an active member of the Arkansas Women's Democratic Club.

5. Vice-President Charles Curtis.

DECEMBER 22, 1931

Sen. Caraway comes to the floor expecting a vote on a bill by Sen. Key Pittman (D-Nev.) proposing emergency construction grants to the states for unemployment relief. Instead the topic is a moratorium on foreign war debts. Sen. Kenneth McKellar (D-Tenn.), Sen. Henrik Shipstead (Farmer-Labor-Minn.), Sen. Hiram Johnson (R-Cal.), Sen. Elmer Thomas (D-Okla.), and Sen. Thomas P. Gore (D-Okla.) express opposition, as does Sen. George W. Norris (R-Neb.), who insists the same privilege should be extended to farmers unable to repay their loans from federal farm land banks. Sen. Samuel Shortridge (R-Cal.), Sen. John J. Blaine (R-Wisc.), and Sen. Cameron Morrison (D-N.C.) support President Hoover's proposed moratorium. After an unusually long twelve-hour session, the moratorium is

*passed, sixty-nine to twelve. Sen. Caraway votes with the mi-
nority opposing it, a vote that later proved to be extremely
popular in her campaign for reelection.*

Came over, just getting in in time to answer quorum call. A few
bills introduced and now Johnson is off again on an oratorical
outburst.

Met Mrs. Harrison[1] outside. Went to lunch room with her, but
I had already et. Had a cheese sandwich and cup of coffee in the
office. Came back because I heard a ghost bell, as I thought, calling me. Perhaps to vote on Pittman. Found McKellar making a
long speech. Senator Shipstead went on record. Senator Thomas
now speaking. I wish I knew how I was going to vote. One minute
I'm for one side the next just the opposite. The arguments are not
convincing—for—And I'm sorry I cannot make up what passes
for my mind. Senator Shortridge is holding forth at shorth so he
says. As to California—the sun reluctantly sets.[2] 6:25 P.M. and
we are still here. Mr. Blaine is speaking quite loudly, tho the galleries are nearly empty. Saw Mrs. Moses.[3] She's all packed up to
go home, and worrying over maybe having to wait another day.
At 7:30 P.M. Senator Blaine still talking. Says moratorium has
only 6 months more to run. And asks what will be done then.
Really he seems to be going to talk until the 6 months are up.
Then if it is ratified will it be for 1932-3 or will we need to vote?
Parliamentary Question Mr. President.

Ten minutes to Eight and I haven't ate. They seem almost ready
to vote. Gore is now talking.

It is now 9:30 P.M. Now they are all discussing Farm relief as a
part of the Moratorium.[4] Really seriously, when I know Senator
Norris was facetious and sarcastic only in his speech. Just the
bad little boy trying to put the other fellow in the hole, when he
couldn't have his own way. Senator Morrison was more scared
than I'd have been I believe—and so far off the subject—or the
grasp of the subject I almost had hysterics especially when I saw
the look of awe on Senator Norris face. And they say women talk
all the time. There's been a lot of "old womans' talk" here tonight
—but *I* haven't done any of it.

1. Wife of Sen. Pat Harrison (D-Miss.).

2. A reference to Sen. Hiram W. Johnson (R-Cal.) who managed the lengthy debate against the moratorium.

3. Wife of George H. Moses (R-N.H.).

4. Sen. Huey Long later made the most of Sen. Caraway's vote against the moratorium in one of his Caraway campaign speeches: "Mr. Hoover he got him up this moratorium thing, and the Republican leaders sugar-coated it and the Democratic leaders painted it pink and made it look so good and sweet I swallowed the dadblamed thing—hook, line and sinker—when I didn't really know but what a moratorium was something about burying people. . . . And every last one of us down in this neck of the woods fell for that thing, all but one—and that was the little woman senator from Arkansas. She said, 'Nay, Nay!' when they wanted her to sign on the dotted line. She said: 'If you want to take $270,000,000 and give it to the farmers, I'll vote for that, but I won't vote to give it to the Wall Street bankers.' And all of us smart men have been kicking ourselves ever since because we can see now that if we'd 'a' had the sense of a last year's bird nest, we would have followed her lead." Quoted by Hermann B. Deutsch, "Hattie and Huey," *Saturday Evening Post*, October 15, 1932, p. 92.

JANUARY 4, 1932

Greetings are exchanged after the Christmas recess, and the Senate begins consideration of S.J. Res. 60, authorizing the distribution of government-owned wheat to the needy through charitable organizations, with supporting speeches by Sen. Kenneth McKellar (D-Tenn.) and Sen. Robert B. Howell (R-Neb.). Additional inconclusive votes are taken on the office of president pro tempore.

Late getting in so had to be called in quorum call.

Several came and spoke quite cordially. Sen. Robinson came around for only a moment and at the instigation of Mr. Biffle.[1] Sen. Lewis not here yet. I'm afraid he's sick. I rode over with Sen. Shortridge. Senators Burns, S.C., Hull, Tenn., Harris Ga, Wheeler, whom I called Bryan, etc. are the ones who spoke to him—& Sen. King.[2] Today I almost made the front page as I lost the hem out of my petticoat. A better proof that I'm old fashioned than the false story of my high top button shoes (for shame Mr. Helm.)[3]

The Senate force can meet most any emergency. A needle and black thread were forthcoming and I soon had the damage mended. However from the size of the needle I'm sure it was for sewing on buttons for mere males. McKellar & Howell are talking help for the unfortunate. None can talk with the fire Dad did when he was fighting for ours. Voted again for Sen. Pittman, twice.

Adjourned a few minutes past four.

Had chicken gumbo, oysterettes and coffee sent up from cafe in office building.

1. It is interesting that from the beginning Sen. Caraway feels an estrangement from her colleague Joe Robinson, noting that he only came to greet her at the insistence of his assistant, Leslie Biffle. She may have known, or sensed, that he was anxious for either Rep. Heartsill Ragon or Vincent Miles, Arkansas' longtime Democratic National Committeeman, to replace her. Like many other senior-junior senators, Robinson and Thaddeus Caraway had a correct but strained relationship: they had clashed over patronage and publicity; Robinson's conservative views often differed from Thad's (and then Hattie's) populistic orientation; and both Caraways lacked the polish and suavity that permitted Robinson's easy entrée into the more sophisticated political and financial inner circles. Several people I interviewed remarked that if Robinson had made a greater effort to cultivate Hattie, she might not have been drawn so easily into Huey Long's orbit.

2. Sen. Caraway clearly feels that Sen. James F. Byrnes (D-S.C.), Sen. Cordell Hull (D-Tenn.), Sen. William J. Harris (D-Ga.), and Sen. Burton (not Bryan) K. Wheeler (D-Mont.) are greeting her companion in the Senate subway car, Sen. Samuel M. Shortridge (R-Cal.), rather than herself.

3. William P. Helm of Helm's News Service; this particular story cannot be located in print.

JANUARY 5, 1932

No legislative business is transacted.

Late for quorum call.

Funny prayer. Sen. Black was asked to have read into the record.[1] Think he'd have been crazy to have read it. Buck Hayden[2] called me out. No news. Two interviews yesterday.

1. The prayer, which must have come from a constituent of Sen. Hugo Black (D-Ala.), begins, "O Thou before whose all-searching sight darkness dissolveth like a dream, breathe on us now with lucid morning's fragrant breath the spirit of Thy calm as we embark upon uncharted seas, empurpled and begloomed by clouds of doubt arising from the mists of our thought."

2. Sen. Carl Hayden (D-Ariz.).

JANUARY 6, 1932

The Senate begins consideration, over the objections of Sen. John J. Blaine (R-Wisc.), of S. 1, establishing the Reconstruction Finance Corporation. Sen. Caraway votes against the Longworth amendment to the proposed Twentieth Amendment to the Constitution (which would have restricted off-year sessions of Congress to four-months' duration), but for passage of the joint resolution itself.

Calla[1] came out to office. Miss Younger[2] called. Miss Lane[3] an English newswriter came in. She was very attractive.

Sen. Lewis back and mirabile dictu — he has on a real suit vest — standing collar and black bow tie with a green striped bordered hanky peeping from his pocket. He shows he's been sick in bed. Some discussion on Bill objected to by Blaine. Finally went over. Lovely lunch with Calla and John,[4] for which John paid. Voted no to an amendment to Lame Duck bill. Then Aye on the Bill — Executive Business.

Dad has been gone only two months.

1. Mrs. John Hawthorne, a close friend of the Caraways from Jonesboro.

2. Maude Younger, congressional chairman of the National Women's Party, and a good friend of Hattie.

3. Not identified.

4. Husband of Calla, John Hawthorne, an attorney, was helping Sen. Caraway settle Thad's estate.

JANUARY 7, 1932

At an Agriculture Committee meeting, Sen. George W. Norris (R.-Neb.) apparently dealt rather roughly with Sam Thompson, a nominee to the Federal Farm Board.

Missed quorum call. Interesting Com. meeting. 3 appointees questioned. One Mr. Thompson backed and filled. Any woman, even I, could have done as well even I. He was more nervous when questioned by Norris. I was sorry for him. Probably his appointment will be confirmed but he seems absolutely helpless.

Helen came up—(Mrs. Crean). Of course interested in trying to get a pension of about 100 or 150 per month for her mother.[1] How I wish I knew I'd have 150 per month so long as I shall live. Talked to Joe about the mortgage sale.[2] Adjourned about 4:30.

1. No regular retirement system had been established at this time for civilian or military government employees. Consequently senators and congressmen were under constant pressure to sponsor private pension bills. Here Helen Crean approaches Sen. Caraway about introducing such a bill for her just-widowed mother, Mrs. William J. Nicholson.

2. The Caraways had overextended themselves financially with the purchase of Calvert Mansion, a large and historic home built by Lord Baltimore in 1758. It was heavily mortgaged and had to be sold, a fact of which Sen. Long made excellent oratorical use later that year: "Mrs. Caraway voted with you people and your interests in spite of all the pressure Wall Street could bring to bear. . . . While she was there in the Senate, a-standing by you, the sheriff sold her home for a mortgage she couldn't pay because she didn't have the money. With all the big-bellied politicians in Arkansas campaigning against this one little woman, she stood by you in spite of the fact the sheriff was selling her home over her head. And don't you ever forget that she wouldn't have had to have this home sold. There was an easy road for her to take. Wall Street takes care of its own. But this brave little woman senator stood by you in spite of it." Quoted by Deutsch, "Hattie and Huey," p. 92.

JANUARY 8, 1932

The Senate continues vigorous debate of the proposed RFC and amendments thereto, including one proposed by Sen. Caraway's colorful seatmate, Sen. J. Hamilton Lewis (D-Ill.), permitting equity courts temporarily to enjoin all receiverships and foreclosures that might eventually be rescued by the proposed RFC. Sen. Joseph T. Robinson opposes Sen. Lewis' amendment and submits his own, permitting the RFC further flexibility in its loan-making decisions. Sen. Smith W. Brookhart (R-Iowa) argues that it is farmers who need assistance,

not the banks and railroads designed as the immediate bene-
ficiaries of the proposed agency.

Got down about 8:30. Vinct & Heartsill came over, talked very
little politics.[1] Did get interested in the sale of the house. Said
they would see me tomorrow.

Sen. Lewis is in his mediocre vein—all dressed in red toupe,
pink whiskers—black coat, grey vest and spats. I haven't noticed
the effect & color and tie and hanky to the general ensemble yet
but I'll leave space to put that in.

The newsgatherers caught me in a yawn while my senior senator was making a speech. Sen. Lewis pronounces Arkansas as if it
were "Okkensaw". Many people complimented Sen. L. when he
was through. Brookehart has developed a rather keen sense of
fun, and I like his forceful way of talking. Maybe because I
believe he is honest Brookehart—said he was just as interested in
the farmers in New Hampshire where Sen. Moses can't elect a
single standpatter anymore as in the farmers in Iowa.[2] Recessed.

1. Vincent Miles and Rep. Heartsill Ragon, both being prominently mentioned
as potential candidates for the Senate.
2. Sen Brookhart, denouncing the administration's concern for the railroads
and banks and neglect of the faltering farmers, implies that the surprise election
of a Democratic congressman from New Hampshire in a special election held
January 5 signals the declining popularity even in conservative New Hampshire
of Sen. Moses' philosophy that the economy will improve if everyone just "stands
pat."

JANUARY 9, 1932

After listening to a lengthy response by Sen. Kenneth McKel-
lar (D-Tenn.) to President Hoover's allegations of congressional
extravagance, Sen. Caraway fails to vote on an amendment
making reclamation projects eligible for RFC loans. The result
is a thirty-seven to thirty-seven tie, killing the amendment.
She then votes with a small minority of fifteen for an amend-
ment by Sen. Wesley L. Jones (R-Wash.) authorizing ships and
shipping lines to receive RFC loans.

Another letter from a fool in California. Nuts from where the nuts come from. What more could you expect? First invitation to White House this season.

McKellar is talking entirely too much unless he were saying more. It is now 20 past 12. I'll time him. I refused to vote on an amendment and it was a tie giving the V.P. a chance to vote. I failed to time Sen. McKellar.

Guess I should have voted. The V.P. said "no vote." On the Jones Amendment—I voted aye. Guess I'll have to get a system —Aye one amendment, nay, the next—Frankly I think there will be nothing much for our people anyway.

Sen. Bailey[1] reminds me in some full face views very much of Paul's friend John Couthe.[2]

Adjourned at about 5 P.M.

1. Sen. Josiah W. Bailey (D-N.C.).
2. A young friend of Sen. Caraway's eldest son Paul.

JANUARY 11, 1932

After hearing Sen. Robert F. Wagner's (D-N.Y.) speech on the extensive and precarious relief system in New York City, the Senate resumes consideration of S. 1. Numerous amendments are proposed and debated, including one by newly elected Sen. Edward P. Costigan (D-Colo.) to ensure that no RFC loans could be made to institutions in which RFC directors held interests. Sen. Hugo Black (D-Ala.) proposes an even stronger substitute, which Sen. Costigan accepts, but the Senate defeats, thirty-eight to thirty-two. Sen. Caraway, despite the previous day's experience, does not vote on this amendment but does vote for final passage of the bill itself (it passed sixty-three to eight).

Received Mrs. Rushmore Patterson[1] who invited me to a "Dry" Luncheon in N. Y. purely for publicity for their organization.

Sen. Wagner making speech on hard times in N. Y. City. 12:13 P.M. Didn't speak long. Much discussion of agricultural loan.

Costigan making a speech—offering an amendment to Emergency Financing of railroads and banks. If it is his maiden effort I'd enjoy it more had he waited until tomorrow as I'm hungry and tired. Mr. Couch, and Mr. Moses[2] called. Mrs. Driver and Mrs. Fuller came too—also Mary Gaylord and Mrs. Tomlinson.[3] Mrs. Gaylord surely has grown fat—and ugly—Tho I've never thought her funny.

Mr. Costigan did not write his speech, or his eyes are bad, or the light is bad—because he stumbles terribly. He may be very smart—but really I wish he'd just had his remarks extended in the Record. Mr. Black asked "Will the gentleman yield?" and Mr. Costigan really jumped. Mr. Black's suggestion to Mr. Costigan was by far the most involved I've heard, or I'm just not bright.[4]

1. Mrs. Patterson of New York City led the Allied Women sector of the Allied Forces for Prohibition.

2. Harvey C. Couch, one of the most prominent and prosperous citizens of Arkansas, was founder and president of the Arkansas Power and Light Co. and later added railroads to his empire as well. He had been a political and financial backer of Thad and by some accounts was highly instrumental in securing Hattie's original appointment from Gov. Parnell. C. Hamilton Moses served as his chief legal advisor. President Hoover had enlisted Couch's aid in lobbying Sen. Robinson and Sen. Caraway for passage of the farm credit bill.

3. The wives of Arkansas congressmen William J. Driver and Claude A. Fuller with, possibly, Marian Gaylord, a Hot Springs friend of the Couches, and with the wife of George A. Tomlinson of the U.S. Railroad Administration.

4. In fairness, the legislative situation has now become extraordinarily complicated with insertions in various clauses of conflicting substitute motions.

JANUARY 12, 1932

The Senate has moved on to the farm credit bill, providing additional capital for federal land banks to loan to distressed farmers.

Better day than usual. Sen. B. suggests my bust in capital some day.[1]

1. There is no way of knowing which of the fourteen "Senator B.'s" made this suggestion, but it never materialized.

JANUARY 13, 1932

Sen. Caraway becomes the first woman elected to the Senate.

Latest vote—Caraway 14,121—Carson 436—Floyd 925.[1] Many congratulations. Everyone was most kind. Auntie came over. Left before adjournment.

1. Final returns gave Sen. Caraway 31,133, Sam Carson 1,095, and Rex Floyd 1,752.

JANUARY 14, 1932

Having left early the preceding day, Sen. Caraway finds the Senate had decided to recess for a day so that committees might work on pending legislation.

Answered many telegrams. Some letters. Came over to find everything deserted—which shows the kind of senator I am. Many men was caught off base in same way, which is some consolation. Saw two newspaper men. Almost a run in with Garrett—because he wants to let me in for too much publicity. Went downtown. Saw Mrs. Ayres of Kansas and Mrs. Vestal.[1] She was horrified when she found Rex Floyd was my opponent. "*He* owes everybody in Washington" was her comment. Bought gloves—and some plated flatware. Was terribly tired and hungry when we got home. I am sorry not to accept for Womans National Press Club's Annual Dinner. Maybe they will ask me again next year and I live.

1. Wives of Rep. W. A. Ayres (D-Kan.) and Rep. Albert H. Vestal (R-Ind.).

JANUARY 15, 1932

The Senate listens to discussions of S. Res. 120 by Sen. Pat Harrison (D-Miss.) proposing sharp budget reductions and of S. Res. 72 by Sen. Robert F. Wagner (D-N.Y.) proposing an extensive federal construction program to provide work for the unemployed.

Notification & certificate of election not here yet. Many nice letters— a box of candy to Dem. Pages. Appropriation Bill up—I can not vote for it entire—as it carries an appropriation for me.[1] However I shall vote on amendments—and parts of it. Sen. Harrison has bill, which I think is purely political, which is to cut 3 millions[2] off the appropriations for this year. How it can be done, with the bills just passed I can't see. However, I'll see how the cat jumps. Mr. Wagner is now making a big speech, but I don't know what he is supposed to be speaking upon. He's introducing a Senate Resolution to have public works go on, so people may be given employment.

1. "To pay to Hattie W. Caraway, widow of Hon. Thaddeus T. Caraway, late a Senator from the State of Arkansas, $10,000." The same sum was authorized for Elizabeth Morrow, widow of Sen. Dwight Morrow of New Jersey.
2. Actually he proposed a reduction of $300 million. The Senate appears to agree with Sen. Caraway's perception of this proposal as "purely political," and after further amending it to make it even more meaningless ("consistent with the existing obligations of the Government and without impairing the necessary power of the Government to perform its duty in meeting the present financial crisis"), they pass the resolution by voice vote.

JANUARY 16, 1932

In an atypical Saturday session, the Agriculture Committee meets, and the Senate resumes consideration of supplemental appropriations. Most of this entry seems to have been written later, describing a weekend full of company.

Not a very good day. Com. met but took no action. Mrs. Fuller[1] came out—I was on the floor not at all. Spent sometime in the gallery but most in the office. Bill for appropriations went over. Had good food, good conversation, etc. when Mrs. Fuller spent Sat. night with us—Van, Auntie, Jno., Lt. Lee, navy, wife & son— Mr. & Mrs. Ragon—Mrs. Claude Fuller, and Heartsill, Jr. came to see us Sunday.[2] Paul went to a young college mens Dem. Club organization meeting. Found it to be a really Roosevelt for Pres. clubs. Indigestion was a companion also in the evening.

1. May Fuller, wife of Rep. Claude Fuller (D-Ark.).

2. Van Alexander Wiley, who lives with Sen. Caraway's sister "Auntie"; "Auntie's" son John; Lt. Lee and family not identified; Arkansas Rep. and Mrs. Heartsill Ragon; wife of Arkansas Rep. Claude Fuller; the Ragons' son Heartsill, Jr.

JANUARY 18, 1932

Sen. Caraway is visited by lobbyists, does some lobbying of her own, exchanges quips with Sen. Robert M. La Follette, Jr. (R-Wisc.), and listens to a lengthy argument among Sen. James Couzens (R-Mich.), Sen. Robert F. Wagner (D-N.Y.), and Sen. Royal S. Copeland (D-N.Y.) over a proposed amendment authorizing municipalities to receive loans from the proposed RFC.

Busy morning. Anti Saloon leaguers. Cotton Association Pres. from Memphis. Sen. Brock, and newspaper relative.[1] Mrs. Abbott, and Dr. Garrison.[2] I called Joe's office to urge him to help on Rural Sanitation Bill. He was very nice. Bankhead back.[3] Sen. Lafollette suggested I'd have to get a flashlight to shine enough for the Vice President to see me. I asked him if he were trying to say that was only way I could shine in the Senate. He disavowed any intention of making such a statement. Mrs. Abbott & I had chicken gumbo, cheese sandwiches and coffee in the office. Sen. Couzens & Wagner & Copeland spat over N.Y. City government living beyond his income.[4]

Auntie & John gone to see Dr. She's very low in spirits. Went home early.

1. Former Sen. William E. Brock (D-Tenn.); newspaper relative not identified.

2. Dr. C. W. Garrison, Arkansas's chief public health official as secretary of the state board of health.

3. Sen. John H. Bankhead (D-Ala.).

4. New York City had by this time spent $32 million for welfare relief, raising $20 million from private contributions and borrowing the rest. New York banks are now demanding immediate repayment and insist that the city increase the subway fare from five to ten cents to cover the cost.

JANUARY 19, 1932

During continued Senate debate on the supplemental ap-
propriations bill, Sen. David I. Walsh (D-Mass.) reports he is
receiving angry letters from constituents protesting the gen-
erous $10,000 payments to widows of deceased members of
Congress, plus payment for funeral expenses. After a brief
discussion, the matter is dropped, but this episode must have
been extremely embarrassing for Sen. Caraway.

Deficiency appropriation still up. Sen. Walsh spoke against
general expenses and years salary to widows, or next of kin.

Went to see Helen & Mrs. Nicholson.[1] Brought home lots of
books. Spurs etc. of Generals.

1. The daughter and widow of Gen. William J. Nicholson.

JANUARY 20, 1932

The Senate Agriculture Committee reports out S. 1234, autho-
rizing an emergency appropriation for special study of and
demonstration work in rural sanitation, but takes no final
action on S. 1856 providing for the relief of farmers through
loans to drainage, levee, and irrigation districts.

Com. meeting—voted favorably the Rural Sanitation bill. Still
no vote on the drainage.

Mrs. Bayard[1] made me a lovely visit. Jim Ham wore a gray suit
and gray felt vest spats to match. Talked to Gen. McArthur about
Paul being sent to Phillippines.[2] Said he had already revoked said
ruling.

1. Wife of former Sen. Thomas F. Bayard, Jr. (D-Del.).
2. Gen. Douglas MacArthur, Army Chief of Staff, had apparently anticipated
Sen. Caraway's request that her eldest son not be sent overseas at this time.

JANUARY 21, 1932

Sen. Carter Glass' (D-Va.) furious response to what he considers a slur made the previous day by Agriculture Secretary Arthur Hyde sets off further partisan responses from Sen. Robert B. Howell (R-Neb.) and Sen. Simeon D. Fess (R-Ohio), chairman of the Republican National Committee. Sen. Caraway's Democratic sympathies are clear, as is her strong support of prohibition. After listening to lengthy Senate debate, she joins a large majority in defeating a resolution proposed by Sen. Hiram Bingham (R-Conn.), and defended by Sen. J. Hamilton Lewis (D-Ill.), authorizing state referenda on prohibition or repeal.

Carter Glass speaking had Borah, Moses, Kean, Robinson, Barklay[1] and most of the older members sitting near and giving a flattering attention. I was thrilled to see it. Fess & Glass some spat. Fess is so sleek and insincere—and tries to be so smooth.

Howell made a speech purporting to be answering Glass but entirely foreign to the subject. I'm told Borah sent Glass a note in the course of Howell's speech, saying—"Fools walk in" etc.—clever.

Sen. Bingham trying to get some action on repeal. Sen. Lewis now serving notice he's to speak on constitutional rights of states to local self government etc. Ate no lunch, had indigestion and took soda. Am terribly sleepy just now.

Conferees report on Federal Land Banks agreed to.[2]

Tydings making a fool speech on the 18th Amendment repealed[3] —Oh yeah!

Brookhart said Bingham's amendment was like a dog chasing his tail.[4] More pure bunk to the square inch today than I have seen. Bingham admits he doesn't know when he is making himself and the Senate ridiculous.[5] Blaine trying to speak for wets.[6] He has to speak on everything anyway. Let the States themselves, whose people are so wet appeal for a Referendum & recall. Maryland recalled Sen. Bruce.[7] Sen. Blaine said all he had to say, then repeated it twice. Senate adjourned over till Monday, and I was awfully glad.

1. Referring to these senators: William E. Borah (R-Idaho), George H. Moses (R-N.H.), Hamilton F. Kean (R-N.J.), Joe T. Robinson (D-Ark.), and Alben Barkley (D-Ky).

2. Final passage of H. R. 6172 providing $125 million additional capital for the federal land banks.

3. Sen. Millard E. Tydings (D-Md.) proposes a constitutional amendment for repeal of the Eighteenth Amendment (prohibition) under which those states refusing to ratify could stay dry.

4. Sen. Smith W. Brookhart (R-Iowa) comments that "the resolution petitions the governors of states to petition the legislatures of the States to ask the people of the States to petition the Senate of the U.S. It is just like a dog chasing his own tail."

5. Actually Sen. Hiram Bingham says he regrets that the Senate has chosen to treat his proposal as though it were ridiculous.

6. Sen. John J. Blaine (R-Wisc.) argues for Sen. Bingham's proposal.

7. United States senators cannot be recalled. However former Sen. William C. Bruce (D-Md.) was not reelected in 1928, having thoroughly antagonized both wets and drys by slipping an amendment into an appropriation bill providing $256 million to the Prohibition Bureau, enough for a genuine enforcement effort.

JANUARY 25, 1932

Sen. Huey P. Long (D-La.) officially enters the Senate, which this day is discussing a proposal restricting to very small sums the salaries of any corporation officials who receive RFC loans. Several senators argue that this is outrageously radical legislation with communist overtones, and it is soundly defeated; but Sen. Caraway and Sen. Long vote with the few supporting it.

Company kept me so long I missed seeing Sen. Long take the oath. I'm sorry.

Wheeler making a free silver speech.[1] Mr. Halsey brought me Magazine section of N.Y. Times of Sun. Jan. 24th.[2] I hope I can keep it. Very nice article. Auntie had luncheon with me. Oysters and pie and coffee. Mr. Long has had his picture made every five minutes and never still. Oh well he will stew and fret. Said it was first speech he'd heard in months that wasn't about him. How uninteresting these speeches will be.

1. Sen. Burton K. Wheeler (D-Mont.) pleads at length for one of his favorite proposals, the remonetization of silver.

2. Edwin A. Halsey, secretary to the minority, brings Sen. Caraway a copy of R. L. Duffus' "A Woman Treads New Paths As Senator," New York Times Magazine, January 24, 1932. One of the few articles that pleases Hattie, it stresses her previous domestic rather than political interests and her diligent efforts to learn the unfamiliar Senate ropes. Interestingly, since the article was based on a lengthy interview, Duffus states that "she was invited to make an agreement not to run again next Fall for the full six-year term. This promise she refused to give."

JANUARY 26, 1932

Sen. Carter Glass (D-Va.) continues his verbal feud with the Agriculture Secretary Arthur Hyde; the Senate begins debate on S. 7 providing for the deportation of certain alien seamen; and Sen. Caraway continues to observe closely her new seatmate, Sen. Huey Long.

Mrs. Norris[1] came to see me. I was so glad to see her. Late to Senate. Met McManus of "Jiggs and Maggie" fame.[2] Told him he taught me the only real use I ever had for a rolling pin. Carter Glass speaking again in reply to Secretary Hyde very clever. Especially quotation about turnip.[3] Quite good. Mr. Long arose addressed the chair in a loud voice — and asked Mr. King[4] the most ordinary question. He has good voice and perfect stage presence. Much discussion on Alien Seamen Act. Did not adjourn — recessed.

1. Wife of Sen. George W. Norris (R-Neb.).
2. George McManus, writer of the popular comic strip "Bringing Up Father."
3. Sen. Glass quotes at length Henry Arthur Jones' reasons for never again pursuing a dispute with H. G. Wells, concluding, "I had wasted a good hour arguing with a turnip."
4. Sen. William H. King (D-Utah).

JANUARY 27, 1932

Sen. Caraway listens to speeches by Sen. Hiram Bingham (R-Conn.) and others opposing Sen. William H. King's proposed alien seaman act but does not stay for the executive session to consider presidential nominations to the executive branch.

Bingham made a speech. He is so insincere it will always be hard for me to vote with him. Leslie talked to me about standing for reelection.[1] Much discussion of Alien Seamen Act. King in charge. Didn't come over for executive session. Some voted against Humphries for Fed. Reserve Board.[2]

1. The Duffus article (see journal entry for January 25, 1932, n. 2), may have prompted Sen. Joe Robinson to send his aide, Leslie Biffle, to Sen. Caraway for clarification of her future plans.
2. Actually the debate involved President Hoover's nomination of William E. Humphrey to the Federal Trade Commission. The nomination is opposed by twenty-eight Democrats and progressive Republicans on the grounds that his prior position as a lobbyist for the lumber industry ill suits him as a regulator of this and other businesses.

JANUARY 28, 1932

Since the Senate usually convenes at noon, there is time for shopping and committee meetings before the day's debate begins. Of most concern to Sen. Caraway this day is Senate discussion of President Hoover's nominees to the RFC board of directors.

Got down 8:30. Went to town bought towels, napkins and hand towels. Paid too much for them. Took Bob[1] to lunch. Huey Long gone back to La. Bankhead[2] a nuisance in Agriculture Com. Fess talking on bimetalism.[3] Talked to Sen. Norris about Mr. Couch's appointment. Both of us cried.[4]

Blaine talking against confirmation Dawes — Couch & Jones.[5] darn it.

1. Robert Easley Caraway, Sen. Caraway's youngest son, at this time a high-school senior, living at home.
2. Sen. John H. Bankhead (D-Ala.).
3. Sen. Simeon D. Fess (R-Ohio) argues at length with Sen. Burton K. Wheeler (D-Mont.) as to whether President McKinley favored the free coining of silver.
4. Apparently Sen. Caraway's conversation with Sen. George W. Norris (R-Neb.) brings back poignant memories of Sen. Thad Caraway's friendship with Harvey Couch (see journal entry for January 11, 1932, n. 2). Couch headed Red Cross relief

work in drought-stricken Arkansas in 1927 and made a very favorable impression on Secretary of Commerce Herbert Hoover, who has now nominated Couch to be a director of the newly established RFC.

5. Sen. John J. Blaine (R-Wisc.) argues unsuccessfully against all three of President Hoover's nominees to the RFC board: Charles G. Dawes, Harvey C. Couch, and Jesse H. Jones.

JANUARY 29, 1932

Sen. Caraway reports on her first meeting of the Senate Library Committee, which at that time considered bills authorizing the construction of federal memorials.

1st meeting Library Com. to pass on fountain for Chevy Chase Circle etc. Also the matter of Analostan Island as memorial to Roosevelt.[1] Moore[2] of Fine Arts Commission angered me by laughing, or sneering about the memorial to Wilson. Said the Fine Arts Commission approved many things that never materializes — I was furious. Stayed down for Paul and answered several letters.

1. Analosta Island in the Potomac River was purchased by Congress in 1931 as a site for a memorial to President Theodore Roosevelt.
2. Charles Moore, chairman of the Commission of Fine Arts.

JANUARY 30, 1932

No session. Stayed at home and swept and put away things.

JANUARY 31, 1932

Fried chicken and strawberries. Van[1] and Auntie came out bearing gifts. Van a vase — Auntie a Japanese garden. Mr. & Mrs. Powell[2] came out.

1. Van Alexander Wiley who lives with "Auntie."
2. Mr. and Mrs. Powell not identified.

FEBRUARY 1, 1932

A memorable day for Sen. Caraway: she celebrates her birth-
day, sells her home, and is officially sworn in to complete the
Senate term ending March 1, 1933. The Senate briefly stops
its business for this purpose but makes no official recognition
of its first elected female member.

My 54th Birthday. Lovely flowers from office force and John
Abbott. Also violets from Stasia.[1] The House sold. Mrs. Roberts[2]
gave me pearls. 3 hankies & face powder. Also took me to lunch.
Mr. Couch called up and wanted to escort me to White House
tomorrow night, to dinner for the Garners.[3] Of course I would not
go, even had I been invited. Stopped Lafollette's speech and was
sworn in.[4] Credentials just came, so thought could just as well be
sworn on my birthday. Award from "Evening in Paris" for being
first woman elected to the Senate. Very nice.

1. "Stasia" was a pet name for a friend of Forrest, the entire nickname being
the Grand Duchess Anastasia.
2. Not identified.
3. Harvey Couch (see journal entry for January 11, 1932, n. 2) invites Sen. Caraway to a White House dinner honoring Rep. John Nance Garner (D-Tex.) who was
elected Speaker of the House on December 7, 1931.
4. Sen. Robert M. La Follette, Jr. (R-Wisc.), yielded briefly before beginning a
speech on unemployment legislation.

FEBRUARY 2, 1932

Sen. Caraway's pleasure over her new role of honor continues,
as does her grief for "Dad." It is interesting that although she
is now a senator, she still is regularly invited to, and usually
attends, the Tuesday luncheons of congressional wives.

Lee Wilson[1] called. Mrs. Broussard[2] for Hostess Com. asked
me to the luncheon. I am glad I went. Everyone was lovely. The
food was good too. Kenneth Watson[3] came in—wants job—as

do they all. Told Mrs. Moses Mr. Moses made me swear yesterday.[4] Said I'd rather be sworn in than sworn at. I sat in seat of
honor, unusual for me. Mrs. Nicholson came up—showed her my
office. She wept over Dad's picture. Mrs. Keane[5] thought the picture lovely. The Evening in Paris program gave me the award for
achievement for women on Mon. night. The present hasn't come.
Hope it will.

1. Robert E. Lee Wilson, multimillionaire of Wilson, Arkansas, owner and oper-
ator of the largest farming operation in Arkansas, had been an honorary pallbearer
for Thad Caraway.
2. Wife of Sen. Edwin S. Broussard (D-La.).
3. A friend of Paul Caraway.
4. Sen. George H. Moses (R-N.H.), as president pro tempore of the Senate, officially administered the oath of office to Sen. Caraway. After repreated inconclusive votes on a replacement for Moses, the Senate had finally voted on January 6
to drop the matter; and according to Senate precedent, a president pro tem continues in office until a successor is elected.
5. Either the wife of Sen. Hamilton F. Kean (R-N.J.) or the wife of Brig. Gen.
Jefferson R. Kean.

FEBRUARY 3, 1932

*The Senate is debating a bill by Sen. Edward P. Costigan (D-
Colo.) and Sen. Robert M. La Follette, Jr. (R-Wisc.) establishing a Federal Emergency Relief Board to administer grants to
the states for unemployment relief. Supporting speeches are
made by Sen. Smith W. Brookhart (R-Iowa) and Sen. John J.
Blaine (R-Wisc.). Sen. Hugo L. Black (D-Ala.) and Sen. Huey P.
Long (D-La.) argue for the Black substitute, under which loans
would be administered by the separate states for road construction. Senator Charles L. McNary (R-Ore.), pleased with
the division in Democratic ranks, moves for consideration of
executive business. Sen. Joe Robinson, as minority leader,
tries to ascertain which, if either, of these proposals would
escape President Hoover's veto.*

Got a new pencil. Paul Yates[1] came to see me. Ate three pieces
of candy. He's nice. Costigan making a speech. Has good delivery.

Have just remembered I came up on elevator with Senator Walsh[2] of Montana one day. He got off elevator with his friend first — as of course an older Senator does precede others. However, I was glad because I got just the right light on his back to find that he too wears shiny serge. Shines from sholders to trousers hem. Dad was not only man who economized it seems. Dear old Dad — how much I miss him — and how I do wish he could have stayed. Nothing can really reconcile me in a way. Costigan & Black still talking. Giving McNary and others some pleasure. Also the galleries. Huey made an appointment today with Assistant Secretary of the Navy Jahncke,[3] then went off. The Under Secretary came, left his card and *went.* Hooee!!! Somebody's shirt is torn. Huey says he doesn't give a damn. Senator Lewis saved me copy of magazine section of N.Y. Times that had a write up of me — but I already had it.

The main objection would be that Costigan must finish his speech. He has had it in his system for many days. I was glad that Senator Robinson asked the question as to whether he had any assurance that his bill would not be vetoed. I fail to see where one speech taking up nearly one and one half calendar days another taking up probably longer is instead making haste almost too slowly. Why ask White House views, when it is life and death to American people to delay. The only thing would be to pass the bill — and serve it up to Sir Erbert to sign, and see that such pressure is brought to bear that he can only veto at *his peril!*

I read somewhere that lightweight clothes add to a speakers ability. Sometimes I wish some of these Senators were dressed in tarleton or gauze. They need something added to their attractiveness as speakers. Sense maybe. Lots of it. Also long windedness. Now Brookhart is up. And Blaine is soon going to erupt. Huey the dynamic Governor has taken the whole thing in hand and how he tries to talk them down. Oh, boy! Blaine is up now, God help us. Costigan is resting. This will probably go on a week. Woe, Woe, Woe!

1. Paul C. Yates, Washington correspondent for the *Arkansas Gazette.* Sen. Caraway usually offered candy to her callers.
2. Sen. Thomas J. Walsh (D-Mont.).

3. Ernest Lee Jahncke, Assistant Secretary of the Navy and a frequent adviser of President Hoover.

FEBRUARY 4, 1932

By this time the Federal Farm Board had exhausted both its capital and its confidence, and the Agriculture Committee was considering legislation to dissolve it.

Com. meeting on abolishing the farm board. Interesting. No lunch—just candy. Prize for Evening in Paris came. It is really very lovely. I feel badly to accept so handsome a gift. Went downtown. Bought black petticoat. My sale[1] not until tomorrow. Senate adjourned early. Forrest came to supper.

1. Official closing on sale of her house, Calvert Mansion.

FEBRUARY 5, 1932

Sen. Edward P. Costigan (D-Colo.) is still arguing for his unemployment relief bill, insisting that federal grants for this purpose are both constitutional and necessary.

My 30th Wedding Anniversary. And Dad has been gone nearly 3 months. No one will ever know how much we miss him. Went downtown. Got some lovely china cheap. Some for Auntie. She, Miss Pike, some other girl—Pearl, John, Garrett and I all had clam chowder together.[1] Made first remarks in Com. asking Senator Bankhead some questions.[2] He rather worries me. The more some people talk the less they say. He's all right, but we can not see eye to eye.

> To empty seats he waxes bold
> And cries aloud in woe
> For Mankinds ills, and coughs, and cold
> But this we all must know.

If they're as starved and thinly clad
And is their want so dire,
While he rehearses cases sad
From hunger they expire.

Written on floor of Senate while Mr. Costigan spoke to empty seats, with gestures on February 5th 1932.

1. Miss Pike not indentified; with Pearl (Mrs. Garrett) Whiteside, John Abbott, Garrett Whiteside.
2. Sen. John H. Bankhead (D-Ala.).

FEBRUARY 8, 1932

A day dominated by two very lengthy speeches: a dissertation by Sen. Cordell Hull (D-Tenn.) on the relationship between high tariffs and depressed farm conditions, given while Sen. Kenneth McKellar (D-Tenn.) presides; and an oration by Sen. Hugo Black (D-Ala.) on the Hamiltonian centralistic philosophy embodied in S. 3045 as compared with the Jeffersonian decentralized approach of his substitute, given while Sen. John H. Bankhead (D-Ala.) presides. Sen. Caraway helps pass the time by exchanging notes with Sen. Marcus A. Coolidge (D-Mass.).

One of the Pages died. I'm so sorry. He had pneumonia, and got a streptococcic infection of his throat. In the midst of life we are in death is certainly true these days.

Mr. Cordell Hull making a political speech. Very poor delivery.

Had lunch. Awful—soup and tomatoes—cofee 35¢, tip 10¢ —making 45 cts. That's pretty bad.

Mr. Black making a rather good speech. Very energetic and much stress and accent.

I notice McKellar presided when his colleagues spoke and Bankhead presides while Black waves his arms and orates. I wrote to Sen. Coolidge—"Will Mr. Bankhead find heaven tame in comparison to the thrill he's getting now? And he wrote, He has reason too. I'm wondering about those two o's in to. Mr. Black has finished his speech but he doesn't know it—and I'm afraid he's fixing to make it all over again. Please sit down Mr. Black!

Adjourned, or recessed rather early.

FEBRUARY 9, 1932

Sen. John H. Bankhead (D-Ala.) accompanies Sen. Caraway to the Senate from an Agriculture Committee meeting. There is further extensive discussion of proposed unemployment relief legislation with Sen. Thomas J. Walsh (D-Mont.) and Sen. Robert J. Bulkley (D-Ohio) arguing for their substitute— expanded public works construction programs to be administered by state governments.

Came over with Senator Bankhead again. Saw Grady Miller[1] in the office. He was very nice. Sen. Walsh discussing the substitute for the Costigan Lafollette bill. I read the cutest clipping from Benton Co. Ark. paper. Want to show it to Sen. Norris. Sent clipping to Brookhart and Norris[2]—Shouldn't I guess.

Gov. Brough[3] came to see me.

Drew likeness of Bulkley—He's speaking now on a subject already talked to death—and his delivery is *so* bad.

My first Executive Session.

Very interesting. Galleries all empty. Press men all out. Everyone lolling in his seat and smoking or not as he wished.

1. Charles G. (Grady) Miller, Sen. Joseph T. Robinson's brother-in-law, then employed as clerk to the Conference Minority of the Senate.
2. Clipping unidentified, but perhaps a jab at the stand-pat Republicans, which would have pleased insurgents George W. Norris (R-Neb.) and Smith W. Brookhart (R-Iowa).
3. Charles H. Brough, former governor of Arkansas (1917-1921), who soon entered the Senate race.

FEBRUARY 10, 1932

The Senate hears today primarily from opponents of proposed relief legislation: Sen. Simeon D. Fess (R-Ohio) and Sen. David A. Reed (R-Pa.). Sen. William Borah (R-Idaho) and Sen. George

W. Norris (R-Neb.) delight Sen. Caraway by challenging Sen. Fess' logic in opposing "the dole" for individuals but supporting it for banks (the RFC).

Interviewed again and sorry of it. Came over as early as usual Heard Will Rogers[1] was in reception room. Went out. Gov. Brough[2] was there. Danced me over to meet Will Rogers. I told him one of the last things Dad chuckled over was his saying Gov. Hoover had appointed a commission to find out whether he had died or not. They both laughed. Newsman came and got our pictures. Me standing between Will and Sen. Robinson. Woman—Mrs. Powell wants me to eulogize Mrs. Susan B. Anthony on Monday—nix on that.[3]

Fess is talking against any help to anyone. He and Norris got sort of het up. Really Fess is unbearable. He is insincere. Not truthful and quite vociferous. A real nuisance, but a good man for Hoover because he has no principles he can not scrap at a moment's notice. Reed has a boil on his neck—but he can still talk for Hoover.

Poor Fess—He seems to be talking on every side of the question.

Borah now—as usual Borah was picturesque and plausible. Skinned Fess which pleased me. Sen. Norris in his best vein on the appointment of Mellon to St. James. Exec. Sess. Norris said of Mellon was most notable Sec. of Treas. this country has ever had —because *three* different Presidents have served under him.[4]

1. Will Rogers, popular American humorist. In thanks to Arkansas for giving him what he called his finest possession, his wife Betty Blake of Rogers, Arkansas, he had made a four-day tour of the state in 1931 with all proceeds going for drought relief work.

2. See journal entry for February 9, 1932, n. 3.

3. Mrs. Powell not identified; Susan B. Anthony died in 1906 after leading the women's suffrage movement for more than fifty years.

4. Andrew W. Mellon had served as Secretary of the Treasury since 1921. Increasingly unpopular as the economy continued deteriorating, President Hoover decided to make him ambassador to Great Britain (the Court of St. James), replacing Charles Dawes who returned to head the RFC. Regular Republicans lauded him as "the Greatest Secretary of the Treasury since Alexander Hamilton" for having served under three different presidents. Progressive Republicans agreed with Sen. George Norris, who caustically observed, "He has had the honor of having three Presidents serve under him."

FEBRUARY 11, 1932

*Sen. Caraway again versifies her observations. The first poem
refers to the earlier-described incident when Sen. George H.
Moses described insurgent Republicans as "Sons of the Wild
Jackass"; the second refers to the continued debate between
those favoring the direct relief bill proposed by Sen. Edward
Costigan and Sen. Robert La Follette, Jr., and those favoring
the more conservative substitute proposed by Sen. Hugo
Black and Sen. Robert J. Bulkley.*

Spent night with Auntie. Much good food. Rumors we are to go
over until Monday so that observe Lincoln's birthday. Hope so.
Costigan speaking. Many others. Saw the Will Rogers pictures.[1]
Autographed one. "To my friend the Senatoress. Will Rogers." *Of
course* I'll keep it. Met the Governor of Utah as we came up on
the elevator with him and Senator King.[2] (The following written
after 1st week in Senate. Copied here to preserve for the world.)

> *Mr. Moses made a really wise crack*
> *When he dubbed them the sons of a jack*
> > *Of the wild ass variety*
> > *Now in all sobriety*
> *He'd much like to take it all back.*
> *They all have their heels in the air*
> *Each and every refusing a pair*
> > *They vote every day*
> > *In just the same way*
> *And tell him to go take the air.*
> *Now when it's all over and done*
> *If the Sons of the Jack haven't won*
> > *Will the gal in the Senate*
> > *Be labelled a jennet*
> *God forbid such a horrible pun.*

Written when Black-Bulkley substitute offered to Costigan-
LaFollette bill.

They came and talked for days & days
Depression for to shoot
But all they got, the V.P. says
Was just a substitute,
A substitute to the bill on hand
With speeches long and loud
Substitutes like grains of sand
Will meet us now on every hand
E'en till I'm in my shroud.
Meanwhile the unemployed can't eat
Their children cry for bread.
Will substitute words for merely meat
And then reiterate and repeat
With substitutes till they're dead.
Sen. Costigan parades with mien most sad
His arguments they refute.
The same comes to the Lafollette lad.
They are offered a substitute.
The substitute I'd like to see
Is down on the Avenue
In the White House there should really be
A man of sympathy true.
We substitute Bills with quite a whack
Wouldn't it be simply grand
If for Herb we could substitute Joe or Jack[3]
Substitute and *demand?*

1. See journal entry for February 10, 1932.
2. Gov. George H. Dern and Sen. William H. King, both Utah Democrats.
3. "Joe" or "Jack" probably refers to Sen. Joe Robinson who had been a vice-presidential candidate in 1928, and to Rep. John Nance Garner (D-Tex.), Speaker of the House, who hoped to be the Democrats' presidential nominee in 1932.

FEBRUARY 16, 1932

After a brief Lincoln's birthday recess, the Senate is still debating S. 3045, the Costigan-La Follette relief bill. Sen. Key Pittman (D-Nev.) urges a realistic compromise to avoid a presidential veto. Sen. Hugo Black (D-Ala.) and Sen. David

Walsh (D-Mass.) argue for their substitute, but Sen. Caraway joins the majority in defeating it, fifty-eight to twenty-eight. She finally joins the minority supporting S. 3045, which is defeated forty-eight to thirty-five, and enjoys the supporting speech by Sen. George Norris (R-Neb.). However, she thinks Costigan, La Follette, and Royal Copeland (D-N.Y.) are over-doing their oratory in its behalf; and Sen. Burton K. Wheeler (D-Mont.) arouses a click of feminist consciousness with his remarks.

Got to office at 8:30. Read papers. Went to Committee meeting on mussel Shoals.[1] Very interesting. Went to Luncheon. Mrs. Bulow[2] very attractive. Sat next Mrs. Sheppard.[3] She asked what the girl who wore red flannel and wool stockings got, and the answer was *nothing.* Sen. Logan[4] after asking if I were an historian, asked if I knew the color of Queen Elizabeth's wedding gown, when she poor thing was never a bride. I only remembered just in time that she was the "virgin queen." Saw Mr. Holmes[5] the news-man. He's nice. Mr. Walsh made a speech against the bill. Costigan talking again. So many of these men look up to the Press Gallery while speaking. Saw Sen. Walsh of Mass. just look up there & smile. Mr. Wheeler now up. (There isn't a man but will say—but what will the *woman* say?)[6] The young LaFollette is fanning the air, and being too dramatic. He is almost persuading me to vote against it. Do wish he would stop. It is his bill, and he's fathering as I mothered my first baby. Everyone must be made to see what a perfect child it is. (Yes, he favors it for the votes his saying so may get him in Alabama). Sen. Black favors taking all the taxes from man of large incomes. In fact the new levies should come entirely from them.

It is now nearly five thirty and Black is out on a flood of oratory and absolutely drunk on his own words he may talk till dawn. I wonder what would happen if I should move to *recess.* It would be awful but I do wish this had been some day when we were not going out to dinner.

Copeland and Costigan have both grandstanded. Pittman is now seeking to delay the vote until tomorrow. After many minutes Now Sen. Norris is speaking. A very good speech. They talk about houses being sold from over your head—and starving. My house has been sold. And I'm really hungry but not like those spoken of in this bill.

I voted for Costigan Lafollette Bill.

1. A group of progressives led by Sen. George Norris of Nebraska had fought unsuccessfully for years for government operation of the Muscle Shoals property on the Tennessee River. Congress had twice passed the bill, but it was twice vetoed by Republican presidents. President-elect Franklin D. Roosevelt became an advocate of an even more ambitious plan encompassing Muscle Shoals, the Tennessee Valley Authority, which was enacted May 18, 1933.

2. Wife of Sen. William J. Bulow (D-S.D.).

3. Wife of Sen. Morris Sheppard (D-Tex.).

4. Sen. Marvel M. Logan (D-Ky.).

5. George Sanford Holmes, Washington correspondent for the *Birmingham Post* and other newspapers.

6. Sen. Burton Wheeler, speaking for the Costigan-La Follette bill, remarked, "I venture the assertion that no man will rise on the floor of the Senate and assert for one moment that the city authorities in any city in the United States are responsible for unemployment in that community."

FEBRUARY 17, 1932

Since only five southern Democrats voted for the Costigan-La Follette bill, its backers were apparently surprised and delighted with Sen. Caraway's support, and here express their gratitude.

Kenneth Watson[1] came down and we had luncheon together. Senators Copeland, Neely, Costigan[2]—Tom Heflin[3] and others congratulated me on my vote. Mr. Bailey[4] says he didn't vote with me—but voted wrong. Got my proofs—pretty good. Bob's especially. Went downtown—bought some plates—cups and saucers—paid too much. Man wanted me to speak over the radio. Am refusing. Made pictures of us on little train—Norbeck—Cutting—Bankhead and someone.[5] I told them I had my picture with Will Rogers last week and now with them and I wondered which would be the funniest.

1. A friend of Paul Caraway.

2. Sen. Royal S. Copeland (D-N.Y.), Sen. Matthew M. Neely (D-W.Va.), and Sen. Edward P. Costigan (D-Colo.).

3. Former Sen. Thomas J. Heflin (D-Ala.).

4. Sen. Josiah W. Bailey (D-N.C.).

5. Sen. Peter Norbeck (R-S.D.), Sen. Bronson Cutting (R-N.Mex.), and Sen. John H. Bankhead (D-Ala.). The little train is the Senate subway car.

FEBRUARY 18, 1932

The Senate has begun debating S. 3616, the Glass-Steagall bill, an effort to increase the circulation of money and thereby inflate the economy through temporary adjustments in certain federal reserve regulations. Sen. Arthur H. Vandenberg (R-Mich.) supports the measure as a modest step in the right direction, but Sen. John Thomas (R-Idaho) thinks its temporary nature will create the short-range illusion of improved finances with more serious long-range consequences.

Arrived early. 8:30. Answered numerous letters. An insurance agent came and wanted us to take out insurance. I was furious for him to get into my office that way. Calla[1] sent papers from home. Agricultural com. meeting—very interesting. First thing that stared me in the face was the news story that my brother was caught in dry net.[2] If he was guilty I'm glad they caught him. If innocent I hope he can prove it. Anyway, "me and Mr. Hoover" both get that kind of publicity.[3] Vandenberg now talking—on the Glass Loan Bank Bill. Went to office et a sandwich and cup of coffee (15 cts). Came back to hear Thomas holding forth and Glass grinning.[4] Glass[5] having Secty of Treasury *knows* he can set everybody right on money and banking. He really is a smart man. Got one ticket—and one on steps for Bob.[6] New York Graphic man wants interview. See him again today. "Golden" (negro)[7] wanted me to go on his bail to get him out of jail for being caught stealing coal.

1. Calla Hawthorne. See journal entry for January 6, 1932, n. 4.

2. A still was discovered by federal agents on Walter ("Dick") Wyatt's Tennessee

farm. He was later (May 7) acquitted of liquor charges in federal district court.

3. President Hoover's brother-in-law, C. Van Ness Leavitt, had been arrested on a liquor charge in November 1931.

4. Sen. Carter Glass may have been grinning at Sen. Thomas' elaborate prelude of praise ("On the basis of a relative comparison a gold dollar beside the distinguished and able Senator would actually appear hollow") before the critical comments began.

5. Sen. Glass served as Secretary of the Treasury from 1918 to 1920 under President Woodrow Wilson and resigned to be appointed to fill a vacancy in the Senate. In 1916, while a congressman, he had formulated the original federal reserve system legislation.

6. Tickets for the upcoming Joint Session Commemorating the 200th Anniversary of the Birth of George Washington.

7. Golden not identified.

FEBRUARY 19, 1932

In connection with continued Senate debate on S. 3616, the emergency credit expansion bill proposed by Sen. Carter Glass (D-Va.), Sen. Hamilton F. Kean (R-N.J.) gives a lengthy history of the federal reserve system, and Sen. John J. Blaine (R-Wisc.) proposes an amendment preventing use of any credit extended under the act from being used in the stock market.

Down Early. Many letters. Saw news man who wanted story for Cosmopolitan. Refused. Mr. Bankhead—and Dr. someone had a little spat in the Committee.[1] Bankhead was really insulting. He might have been more tactful. Came in with Dr. Copeland.[2] Kean of N.J. making a speech. Uninteresting.

McAllister's brother from Conway was here.[3] I liked him. Got a letter from Harry Lee Williams sending bill for $90.00 implying that if I did not pay it would cause them to say I am ungrateful to the Governor.[4] I fail to see the connection. However I'll probably have to pay it. Blaine said there was a clear ambiguity in the bill of Sen. Glass. I asked the Senator (Glass) what a "clear ambiguity" is. He said he could not always follow Sen. Blaine. Saw Mrs. Parkhurst.[5]

1. Sen. Caraway is constantly critical of Sen. John Bankhead's treatment of witnesses before the Agriculture Committee.

2. Sen. Royal Copeland (D-N.Y.) was a practicing surgeon, then health commissioner of New York City, prior to entering the Senate in 1922.

3. Heber L. McAllister, president of Arkansas State Teachers College in Conway, Arkansas.

4. Harry Lee Williams, an Arkansas publisher, formerly of Jonesboro, was a strong supporter of Thad Caraway and originally of Hattie, but later wrote bitterly about her in his *Forty Years Behind the Scenes in Arkansas Politics* (Little Rock, Ark.: Parkin Printing & Stationery Co., 1949), pp. 22-30.

5. Mrs. Parkhurst is not identified.

FEBRUARY 22, 1932

Sen. Caraway enjoys the people-watching opportunities afforded by a joint session of Congress commemorating the two-hundredth anniversary of George Washington's birth, the exchange of jokes with Sen. Morris Sheppard (D-Tex.) and Sen. Charles L. McNary (R-Ore.), and the festive family weekend that followed.

Early for first time. Walked with Sen. Sheppard to the House. Sat in next to the front row. Couldn't see the President. Sara[1] had seat in the Gallery where I could see her. Some of the Washington kin were there. One with the most wonderful hirsute adornment of this day and age. I asked Sen. Sheppard who he was. He said— "He must be Bushrod Washington." Sen. McNary said "No, it is Harry Chinn." Went out on capitol steps but only for a moment. Margot[2] went home with a jar of peach preserves under her arm. Sara and Margot were like two cats on a shed. Evelyn[3] came. Spent Sunday & night. *She is sweet.* Auntie & John came out. Forrest, Bing, Train, Dan, Elizabeth Wheeler.[4] Miss Watson & Mr. Nicholas or son (Jim's friends) and Jim came.[5] We had the green plates and other plates—percolator on table. New cups and yellow cups. Pressed chicken, dressed eggs, whole ham, hot potato boats, hot biscuits peach preserves, hot biscuits and strawberry shortcake. Some spread for poor folks. They played Murder. Forrest the murderer, and Paul the District Attorney. It was a good game.

1. Paul Caraway's friend, Sara Stuck of Jonesboro.

2. Forrest Caraway's friend, Margot Willis of Port Washington, New York.

3. Probably Evelyn Hardy Mounts, secretary of the First Methodist Church of Jonesboro and a good friend of Sen. Caraway's.

4. Forrest's friends Bing Kunzig, William Train, Dan Fahey, and Elizabeth Wheeler, daughter of Sen. Burton K. Wheeler.

5. Friends of Jim Carraway, a relative from the Virginia branch of the family (which spells the name differently).

FEBRUARY 23, 1932

Apparently a large number of Arkansas visitors came to Washington for the George Washington bicentennial festivities, and many called on Sen. Caraway.

Got down to office all worn out. Judge and Mrs. Rose[1] came. They are lovely people. Mr. Kays[2] and 4 men from home. Capt. Eldridge, Mr. Keller, Mr. Rankin[3] and another man came out to dinner. The kids seemed to enjoy it. Mr. Haley[4] and his wife came to see me. They were very very nice.

1. Probably the George B. Roses of Little Rock. He was senior partner in the law firm of Rose, Hemingway, Cantrell and Loughborough, distinguished in his knowledge of fine arts as well as the law, and though never an elected judge, held several brief appointive judicial positions.

2. Victor C. Kays, president of Arkansas State College at Jonesboro.

3. Capt. Eldridge, a teacher of military science at Arkansas College; Gordon Keller, a Jonesboro attorney and judge; Rep. John Elliot Rankin (D-Miss.).

4. Probably the Tom Haleys of Paragould, Arkansas.

FEBRUARY 24, 1932

It is likely that many of the Arkansas visitors wanted to talk politics, leaving Sen. Caraway with anxious thoughts about her future.

Forrest had lunch with me. We edited an interview with Mr. Craven from New York Graphic. Am sorry but I walked into it. Mrs. Roberts[1] came talked to me. Says she might drive me down home when I want to go. Wish she would. Mr. Kays[2] came in again. Surprised at mail we get. Mr. Holmes[3] in office. Awfully nice, liked Forrest and liked my proofs. Life runs on & on. Ambitions rise, are downed and rise again. Oh! Well—I'm going to rock long as sympathetic and consistently as I can and leave the all wise one to show me my path. Surely if I can trust enough and try not to dwell on what I'd *like* to do—then somehow I'll be shown the way, the right way.

1. Not identified.
2. See journal entry for February 23, 1932, n. 2.
3. Ibid., February 16, 1932, n. 5.

FEBRUARY 25, 1932

Sen. Caraway is delighted with the reappearance of Sen. Huey Long but worried about increasing pressure for clarification of her political plans.

Awfully tired but down early. Not many letters for my personal attention. Got thru them. Mrs. Cooper[1] came down to see me. She looks terribly. Has broken her nose. I shall always remember her telling me one time that she takes 3 baths every day. We had lunch. Huey in much perfection sartorially came back. Asked how his pardner was and whether she was true to the Kingfish. Joe brought me a letter from Vint. Miles to read.[2] Guess I said too much or too little. Never know.

1. Probably Mary Cooper, wife of Rep. Jere Cooper (D-Tenn.) of Dyersburg, near Sen. Caraway's hometown.
2. Joe Robinson bringing a letter from Vincent Miles, one of Sen. Caraway's eventual opponents.

FEBRUARY 26, 1932

The Senate is debating S. 932, the proposed Norris-La Guardia anti-injunction act, which would greatly restrict the power of federal courts to issue injunctions against labor unions. The day's discussion is heavily dominated by lawyers discussing legal technicalities, and Sen. William H. King (D-Utah), former associate justice of the Utah Supreme Court, clearly does not appreciate the frequent interruptions by Sen. Huey Long recalling personal experiences as a trial attorney representing workers attempting to organize.

Came over in time to answer roll call. Saw Miss Younger.[1] Let her have two books. "The Battle of the Horizons" by Sybil Thompson and "Old Pylus" by Warwick Dearing. Miss McNamara[2] came and talked to me. Is writing a personal interest story. Very interesting and sympathetic person. She is nice. Sen. Long back. He is so likeable. I really wish he would conform a little more. However, he is so colorful. Is now making a speech on the subject he has not studied. Sen. Logan made a little speech.[3] He is one of my favorites. Joe not here today. King yielded the floor and left the room as Long interrupted him. He is walking in where angels fear to tread. The men from the house came in smiling. It is nice to have a boy tell these people about this thing they have studied for years. He says "whur" and rather butchers his English right much. It is almost laughable how much I resent any flouting of the traditions of the Senate. King yields the whole floor every time Long rises to ask him a question. Adjourned over until Monday.

1. See journal entry for January 6, 1932, n. 2.
2. Miss McNamara and her story not identified.
3. Sen. Marvel Logan (D-Ky) asks questions regarding procedures under the proposed law for enjoining acts of violence.

FEBRUARY 27 — 28, 1932

Home—washed and curled my hair. Mrs. Stubblefield[1] and I plan to drive home soon. Harris & Ewings[2] sent out and made pictures of the whole family—groups and singly. Read Mulfords latest book "Mesquite Jenkins—Tumbleweed." Forrest & Bob do not like it so well. I enjoyed it—and for once refrained from reading the back of the book first. Made candy.

1. A Washington, D.C., real estate agent and good friend of Sen. Caraway.
2. A prominent Washington, D.C., photographic studio. See illustration.

FEBRUARY 29, 1932

In this entry, Sen. Caraway sizes up her potential opposition should she run for reelection: Gov. Harvey Parnell, who appointed her; William F. Kirby, associate justice of the Arkansas Supreme Court, who succeeded James P. Clark to the United States Senate in 1919 but was then defeated by Thaddeus Caraway in 1920; Vincent Miles, long-time Democratic National Committeeman; Melbourne Martin, attorney; Rep. Heartsill Ragon of Clarksville; and O. L. Bodenhamer, businessman and former national commander of the American Legion.

Every day it is more borne in on my consciousness that to try to fill Dad's shoes is a rather large undertaking. I can but think — I did not try to wear the pants while Dad lived — yet I'm trying to fit my feet into his shoes. I can well know they are easier on my feet than they'd be on Parnell's or Kirby's. Dear, dear, I wish I could know what is the course to pursue. None of us can look into the future tho. The way I figure Kirby's backing will be good, but not too popular. He has slipped into Senate once over a dead mans body. Did not prove very well fitted and was repudiated by 50000 votes. Parnell can not claim any promise from me for none of his efforts to buy me succeeded. I refused to make any promises and I can't forgive his heartlessness or the mental agony he must have caused Dad those last days.[1] Vincent has not strength much. Martin is little and unknown. Brough a back number. It would seem Ragan & Bodenheimer have decided not to run. Oh well, I'll drift along and see what happens.

Sara Majors Cook[2] came to see me. I'm sure she wants a job. Seems to have run into a storm on life's sea and is I am sure. Sen. Bulkley said something funny about me to Hayden because Sen. Bankhead was talking to me.[3] How awful that men always think evilly or unkindly. I did say a fool thing to Bankhead — but it was innocently done, and I'm not going to worry. I'll quit talking to them all. Lunched with Mrs. Stubblefield[4] Feb. 29th. Had luncheon last week with Mrs. Blaine.[5]

Robert, Hattie, Paul, and Forrest Caraway, 1932. Harris and Ewings.

1. See introduction.

2. Not identified.

3. Sen. Robert J. Bulkley (D-Ohio), Sen. Carl Hayden (D-Ariz.), and Sen. John H. Bankhead (D-Ala.).

4. See journal entry for February 27, 1932, n. 1.

5. Wife of Sen. John J. Blaine (R-Wisc.).

MARCH 1, 1932

Sen. Caraway is reluctantly preparing to go home, her first trip to Jonesboro since her husband's death. After a series of parliamentary maneuvers, the Senate passes the Norris-La-Guardia anti-injunction bill, and Sen. Caraway joins the majority in voting for adoption.

Mrs. Hayden called on me.[1] Was so glad to see her. Wonderful writeup in Sunday's Gazette Magazine section. Think Charlotte Frierson must have written it.[2] Shall find out when I go home. I dread so to go—but must do it. This following along the lines of least resistance doesn't always pay. Saw Mr. Yates.[3] He wanted to know if I had any political announcement to make. I said *no*. From Shipstead's Desk he is speaking at length today—Thomas, Okla is speaking on another bill than one on the Calendar.[4] "Out of Order" he got unanimous consent to introduce bill and make statement now. He is very tall and straight irregular homely features—rather rugged strength in face & figure. Beautiful wavy white hair, which is receding from his temples more every day. At about the part in his hair. Soon he will be wearing a wide part in the middle without in the least wanting a part there. Mrs. Harrison[5] called up. Reminded me of luncheon, and we sat together. Mrs. Dill and Mrs. Smith.[6] Also Mrs. Lenroot.[7] Cafeteria style. Think they're going back to old way of serving. Mrs. Hayden came to see me. She's lovely. Norris & Blaine[8] having a lovely set to. Mrs. Smith went to office with me. Had some candy & a cigarette and waited but I got tied up. Couldn't come over at once.

1. Wife of Sen. Carl Hayden !D-Ariz.).

2. "Junior Senator from Arkansas," *Arkansas Gazette Magazine*, February 28, 1932, was written under the name Eudocia Lucky by "a friend and former neigh-

bor who for personal reasons prefers to hide her identity under a nom de plume."
Hattie here speculates, probably correctly, that "Eudocia Lucky" is Charlotte
Frierson, wife of Charles Frierson, Jonesboro attorney, who was chairman of the
Craighead County Democratic Committee (and did not support Hattie in the 1932
Democratic primary). This article is discussed in the introduction.

3. Washington correspondent for the *Arkansas Gazette.*

4. Sen. Elmer Thomas (D-Okl.), using the centrally located desk of Sen. Henrik
Shipstead (Farmer-Labor-Minn.), asks the Senate to approve his bill authorizing
immediate payment to World War I veterans of the amounts owed them on their
adjusted-service certificates. By this time, fifty different bills authorizing the so-
called veterans' bonus had been introduced in Congress.

5. Wife of Sen. Pat Harrison (D-Miss.).

6. Wives of Sen. Clarence C. Dill (D-Wash.) and, probably, Sen. Ellison D. Smith
(D-S.C.).

7. Wife of Irvine L. Lenroot, judge of the United States Court of Customs and
Patent Appeals, former United States Senator from Wisconsin.

8. Sen. John J. Blaine (R-Wisc.). proposes amending the Anti-Injunction Act to
impose stiff penalties on hiring detectives and other agents to incite strikes and
violence. Sen. George W. Norris (R-Neb.) is sympathetic to the amendment's purpose but fearful that last-minute changes in the bill will delay or prevent final
passage.

MARCH 10, 1932

*Sen. Caraway apparently enjoyed her visit home but also
seems pleased to be back with her colleagues — Sen. John H.
Bankhead (D-Ala.), Sen. Marvel Logan (D-Ky.), Sen. Edward P.
Costigan (D-Colo.), Sen. Carl Hayden (D-Ariz.), and Sen. Hugo
Black (D-Ala.). The Senate has begun discussing a proposed
national sales tax.*

Got back from Jonesboro at 1 A.M. Paul met me at the train—
very cold and icy. Bad storms on Sunday. One of my bills went
over indefinitely today.[1] I was not expecting it and did not even
hear it. Sen. Bankhead first person I saw from Senate itself. Sen's
Logan & Costigan are so nice. I like them both immensely, as well
as Hayden and Black. Joe has not come to speak to me. The Lindberg baby kidnapping still preempts the front pages.[2] It is an
awful shame.

There's no place like home, and home people. I do feel much
refreshed from having had a visit with them.

Sen. Moses called Dill & McKellar two of the most vociferous (in the Senate), and Walsh (Mont.) one of the most intellectual supporters of the Gov. of N.Y.[3]

Went home early. Joe came over for a little talk. I had so little news.

My Little Rock College Bill reported favorably.[4] Hope it goes through tomorrow.

1. S. 1403, for the relief of Rhetta H. Guild, was reported adversely from the Senate Finance Committee and indefinitely postponed.

2. Charles, the infant son of Col. and Mrs. Charles A. Lindbergh, Jr., had been kidnapped March 1.

3. After speeches by Sen. Clarence C. Dill (D-Wash.), Sen. Kenneth McKellar (D-Tenn.), and Sen. Thomas J. Walsh (D-Mont.) opposing a proposed national sales tax, Sen. George H. Moses (R-N.H.) teasingly suggests that these opponents are attempting to discredit one of the bill's backers, House Speaker John N. Garner, as a presidential candidate to assist their own choice, Gov. Franklin D. Roosevelt of New York.

4. S. 1421, a bill to exempt Little Rock College from payment of $1,400 loss to the War Department for materials destroyed while the college was given over to the use of the Reserve Officers Training Corps (see journal entry for March 28, 1934).

MARCH 11, 1932

While the Senate debates emergency road-building funds and executive authority to abolish government agencies, Sen. Caraway confides some critical thoughts about her colleagues to her journal.

My car battery down. Lots of nice letters. Senate at noon. Auntie came at lunch. Jim Ham Lewis made good speech today.[1] Joe got mad at Bingham.[2] Sen. Logan[3] says there should be an open season on Senators when one should be allowed to shoot them on sight with nothing *less* than a 22—and then if hit in the head no dents would be made. He says many of them are so pompous—and that Joe is both—pompous and *mean*. This is pretty personal little journal, but I will edit before its published —if ever. Doesn't it sound big to think or talk of having something published?

1. Sen. J. Hamilton Lewis (D-Ill.) charges the Hoover administration with hypo-
crisy in preaching economy while expanding the numbers and increasing the
salaries of government employees.

2. Sen. Joseph T. Robinson (D-Ark.) has insisted that a proposed amendment
to the Interior Department appropriations bill is not germane, and the Senate,
voting thirty-four to thirty-two, supports his interpretation. When Sen. Hiram
Bingham (R-Conn.) persists in advocating the amendment, Sen. Robinson shows
his disgruntlement.

3. Sen. Marvel M. Logan (D-Ky.).

MARCH 12, 1932

*This entry is somewhat confusing as, contrary to its implica-
tion, Sen. Caraway was present when the Senate convened at
noon for a brief Saturday session; and although there were
several demands for roll call votes on nominees to the Federal Farm Board, none were actually taken.*

The affairs of the Senate gave way to care of the plumbing.
Had to get new tank. Took all day to get where we could build a
fire in the range. We had several roll calls before we had supper
and several demands for the ayes and nos.

MARCH 13, 1932

Made candy. Had good plain food, which Auntie and John and
Forrest helped us eat. Retired early.

MARCH 14, 1932

*On a dairy-state sponsored bill prohibiting purchases of butter
substitutes by any federal agencies, including St. Elizabeth's
Hospital for the Insane, Sen. Caraway makes a decision based
on simple justice and is both flattered and flustered to be told
that Sen. Huey Long and Sen. Marvel Logan (D-Ky.) followed
her lead.*

Saw newspaper man, or special writer or something. He was
quite nice—and hope he does me proud. Today I voted on whether

to demand butter for inmates of St. Elizabeths. I feel that crazy people have as much right to have butter as sane ones, so I voted for butter instead of oleo. Funny. I couldn't feel as if it were of national importance. Maybe I had not thought enough of the cotton seed products. However not being able to grow cotton and make cost of production I feel not so badly. Had luncheon with Sen. Long. He voted with me on this hope it wasn't wrong for that reason. Sen. Logan says he voted aye too because I did—whew—of course my vote counts.

MARCH 15, 1932

At an Agriculture Committee meeting, there is further discussion by Sen. James F. Byrnes (D-S.C.) and Charlie Barrett, former president of the Farmer's Union, about the moribund Federal Farm Board. Later Sen. Caraway exchanges confidences with Sen. Marvel Logan (D-Ky.).

Agriculture Com. meeting—Jimmie Byrnes discussing abolishing Farm Board. Much talk. Nothing done. Charlie Barrett made poor showing I thought. He wandered and wavered and did not commit himself. Guess many jobs will be created, as there will be $50,000 to make investigation. Forrest coming for lunch with me. Bless his heart—it will be nice to see him. Today is Senate Ladies day too.

I thought my Little Rock College bill would come up today—but not yet[1] I hope all these things get thru the house too. Had lunch with Forrest. Sen. Robinson had the Gerry's, the Pittmans[2]—and some tall white haired man as guests. I'm wondering who man was. Someone Alice Longworth[3] knows well. Had long talk with Sen. Logan. He thinks Johnson[4] a great speaker and very smart. Thinks the republicans have smarter men than we have.

1. See journal entry for March 10, 1932, n. 4.
2. Sen. Joseph T. Robinson's luncheon guests were former Sen. and Mrs. Peter Gerry (D-R.I.) and Sen. and Mrs. Key Pittman (D-Nev.).
3. Daughter of President Theodore Roosevelt and wife of Nicholas Longworth (R-Ohio), former Speaker of the House.
4. Sen. Hiram W. Johnson (R-Calif.).

MARCH 16, 1932

During Senate debate on proposed Interior Department ap-
propriations, in which Sen. Charles L. McNary (R-Ore.) has
proposed a flat 10 percent decrease, Sen. William H. King
(D-Utah) and others deliver scathing attacks on the Interior
Department for its treatment of the Pueblos and Navahos.

Mr. & Mrs. McCutcheon[1] of Blytheville came to see me. Homer
Tatum[2] brought them. Associated Press wants picture of me with
Sen. McNary my first "pair."[3] Asked Huey to autograph my copy
of Tin Pot Napolean.[4] He did not. Mr Kavanaugh[5] came in—
wanted to know if I was running. I said as per usual. Sen. Logan[6]
overheard a Congressman tell Long "Now, damn you don't you
double cross me about that, and Huey said God damn you don't
you talk to me like that." A crazy woman got hold of me today.
Wanted job. Said she lost her fiance and brother in the war. Finally she said if she had not lost her fiance she wouldn't be here, and
if I had not lost my husband I would not be here. I said "That was
not kind. I would rather have him back than any job in the world.
Goodbye!" and walked away. She ran after me and called but I
walked into the Senate chamber, and so she had to go. I am not
unsympathetic, but I will not have people say such things to me.
I asked Huey to autograph the book, but it did not go over big.
He says the man who wrote it is a dope fiend. McKellar is asking
that this bill be reported back to the Senate with the order to
slash all the appropriations 10%. If King would stop talking maybe we could get thru this and get the drainage bill passed.
    Adjourned or recessed at 5 P.M.

1. The McCutcheons owned the Ritz Theater in Blytheville and were influential
in both city and county politics.
    2. Secretary to Rep. William J. Driver (D-Ark.).
    3. When senators know they will be absent, they usually arrange for a pair—an
agreement with another senator, ordinarily from the other party, who will be
present but agrees not to vote.
    4. *The Career of a Tin Pot Napoleon* by John Kingston Fineran (New Orleans,
1932). T. Harry Williams describes this first biography of Sen. Huey Long as follows: "Covering only a part of Long's life, it was violently prejudiced against him
and is interesting chiefly as a revelation of the anti-Long mind." Williams, *Huey
Long* (New York: Alfred A. Knopf, 1969), p. 885.

5. Probably Coburn C. Kavanaugh, former sheriff of Pulaski County, member of the Democratic Central Committee, and later Little Rock postmaster.

6. Sen. Marvel M. Logan (D-Ky.).

MARCH 17, 1932

Sen. Caraway's observations on the feud between Alabama's present and former senators are probably prompted by legislation regarding tariffs on agricultural products before the Senate Agriculture Committee on which both she and Sen. Bankhead serve. Beginning the day's Senate debate, minority leader Joseph T. Robinson, echoed by Sen. Tom Connally (D-Tex.), expresses outrage over a newspaper report that Treasury Secretary Andrew Mellon, as soon as he presents his credentials to the king as newly appointed ambassador to Great Britain, will reopen negotiations on the war debt situation to attempt alleviating the burden on the British.

Got down before 8:30. Read Ladies Home Journal and had a cigarette preparatory to occupying my seat here. Life is a queer thing. Alabama has two Senators, one fighting like a bantam cock against that veteran raven, Tom Heflin for his life. Bankhead is little and bald, with a scrub nose and bushy eyebrows adorning beetling brows, if I know the meaning of the expression "beetling brows." He is overbearing—very quick tempered, stubborn, and lacking in political acumen. He has voluntarily alienated Norris,[1] by getting angry and high handed with him. His expressions of such deep interest in getting cotton for nothing for the Spinners of his State was not conducive to make the agriculturists feel too friendly. To me it was so patently his only course to walk lightly and conciliate all parties in so far as was compatible. Oh, well, a woman on suffrance here may only think, and put in a private journal any thoughts she may have.

Robinson made a short speech on Mellons reported statement in today's Washington Post. Now Connally is talking. Doing pretty well. He really is purely an orator of the old time Methodist or Baptist type. All this as part of my political education. I've said you get education and boredom about fifty-fifty in this "chamber." Connally doesn't know when he is through with an argument. He is to me rather childish and his voice is not good. Connally—says Hoover has backbone of iron and face of stone.[2] I'd always thought him as putty, or plaster of paris (it fits beautifully.)

1. Sen. George W. Norris (R-Neb.).

2. Sen. Connally was paying tribute to Sen. David A. Reed (R-Pa.) for repudiating President Hoover's stand on war debts. "I congratulate him in standing out against his chief, in standing out against his chieftain who has a backbone of iron and a face of stone."

MARCH 18, 1932

After extended consideration of several controversial nominations, the Senate takes up the conference report on the anti-injunction bill, with Sen. Hiram Bingham (R-Conn.) pointing out that the House has deleted a provision that would have guaranteed jury trials for those charged with contempt in "padlock" proceedings involving prohibition. Sen. Huey Long berates the Senate for constantly being distracted into wet-dry debates when the real issue is wealth-poverty.

Answered just a wee bit late. Copeland now speaking. Want to put in the record here & now.[1] On Society page of one of the Sunday papers there were a ½ doz. pictures of Society Leaders with their canine companions. Bob suggested I should have mine with my asinine companions. I said "Who, you and Paul?" he said, "No, I meant the Senate." Senator Bankhead[2] suggests he was not so far wrong either.

Mr. Hickman[3] came down to see me. He is very nice and I much appreciated the nice things he said to me. I wrote two hard letters today—one to Dr. Calver,[4] on death of his mother. One to Mrs. Quin[5] whom I much like—and I know what it is to lose as she has.

Another mixup on nominations. It was quite interesting—and Joe and McNary had words,[6] but it peps things up some. Mr. Bingham talking on prohibition. Long now jumping Bingham. He said, "I see the Senator is looking at the clock—it is 4:15." No one seems to have rushed to Huey to congratulate him. He came home to his seat and I had to say something. It would probably have been better for him, if he had remained quiet longer—but he will probably settle down and do better. Here's hoping so. Went home happy because of no session on Saturday.

1. Sen. Royal S. Copeland (D-N.Y.), protesting President Hoover's nomination of Fred A. Bradley to be district customs collector, inserts quantities of material into the *Congressional Record* questioning whether Bradley, Republican chairman of Erie County, New York, has not consorted too openly with bootleggers to be a reputable customs collector.

2. Sen. John H. Bankhead (D-Ala.).

3. An officer of the Washington, D.C., City Bank who helped Sen. Caraway with the house sale and other financial matters.

4. Dr. George Calver, official capitol physician.

5. Widow of Rep. Percy E. Quin (D-Miss.).

6. Sen. Joseph T. Robinson is provoked by, and tries unsuccessfully to block, Sen. Charles L. McNary's (R-Ore.) request that consideration of Charles A. Jonas as United States Attorney for the Western District of North Carolina be postponed another week.

MARCH 21, 1932

Sen Huey Long, angered by a Washington Post *editorial criticizing his simultaneous service as Louisiana governor and United States Senator, delivers a fiery tirade against the* Post, *the wealthy, the oil companies, and the coalition of Democratic and Republican legislative leaders who are attempting passage of a general sales tax.*

Arrived early. Things went along smoothly for awhile. Then Huey got up and read an editorial in Post of some days ago. He made a perfectly *mad* speech. Being right next him I had to sit thru it. My ear drums suffered. He kept harping on co-e-lation of Leadership, etc. That may more nearly express it—but the word he was using was coalition. Anyway he offered us a silver cup gold lined, because I sat thru it. I said—"oh! Sen. it was worth more than that to us. We were amply repaid."

A noted cartoonist of Guatemala made a crayon sketch of me. It was my first caricature that I've seen—and while not pretty was rather good.[1]

1. George De Zayas' caricature was later used to illustrate George Creel's article on Senator Caraway, "The Woman Who Holds Her Tongue," *Collier's,* September 18, 1937, p. 22.

MARCH 22, 1932

Widespread economy-in-government sentiment and numerous speeches against runaway government spending finally leads to the adoption of Sen. Kenneth McKellar's (D-Tenn.) proposal to resubmit the pending appropriation bill to committee with instructions to cut recommendations by 10 percent. Sen. Caraway supports the proposal but not an amendment proposed by Sen. John J. Blaine (R-Wisc.) to limit the Justice Department's appropriation for prohibition enforcement.

Arrived early. Had a talk with the woman who collaborated with Gaston Means on the Harding Book — The Strange Death of Pres. Harding.[1] She may write me up for Liberty. Hope it won't be too bad.

The Senate has been discussing for several hours the McKellar motion to recommit the appropriation bill for Department of Justice etc. I went to Ladies of the Senate Luncheon. Mrs. Dawes and Mrs. Bruce[2] were there. Mrs. Pittman[3] talks to me a lot and I had place of honor on Mrs. Moses[4] left. Luncheon was quite good. There are so many things are different now. Not only that Dad can never come back, no matter how much one would like to have him. A little difference in status makes more difference to more people than I had realized.

The move of Blaine to cut out the whole appropriation for Prohibition enforcement was killed. I voted *no* real loud. Mrs. Robinson[5] wore such a pretty black sweater suit today. There was finally a vote on the Res. to recommit with 10% cut in all appropriations etc.

1. May Dixon Thacker.
2. Wife of former Vice-President Charles G. Dawes with the wife of former Sen. William C. Bruce (D-Md.).
3. Wife of Senator Key Pittman (D-Nev.).

4. Wife of Sen. George H. Moses (R-N.H.).
5. Wife of Sen. Joseph T. Robinson (D-Ark.).

MARCH 23, 1932

The Senate vigorously debates, and finally rejects, the nomination of Charles A. Jonas to be United States Attorney for the Western District of North Carolina, with supporting speeches by Sen. Thomas D. Schall (R-Minn.) and Sen. Arthur Robinson (R-Ind.), and negative speeches by Sen. Thomas J. Walsh (D-Mont.) and Sen. Cameron Morrison (D-N.C.).

Forrest had lunch. Mrs. Stubblefield[1] too. As usual I ate too much. Mrs. Nicholson and her friend came. I put them in Gallery. Sen Walsh making a speech in defense of Bailey—N.C. on Jonas confirmation. Sen. Borah listening. Schall made a terrible speech his voice awful. Anyone who speaks in a voice like should never be allowed to inflict the public. Especially poor people like me, who listen to learn. It is hard enough to try to absorb knowledge without having my ears assaulted by a voice like that.

Sen. Morrison making a speech against Jonas who is up for confirmation. (Mr. Walsh ought to know whether he did or not and I'm inclined to think the Senate would believe Walsh.)[2]

Of course that a man does not tell the truth would not keep a Rep. of Sen. Robinson of Ind. from voting for his confirmation. Poor Morrison has got so high again he is having trouble to alight. If he had only refused to rise to the bait of Robinson's speech. *Please Stop.* He was not confirmed.

1. See journal entry for February 27, 1932, n. 1.
2. Charles Jonas was elected to Congress from North Carolina in 1928 as a Republican and was defeated for reelection in 1930. When the Nye committee (a select committee to investigate campaign expenditures, headed by North Dakota Republican Sen. Gerald P. Nye) dismissed Jonas' charges of election fraud, Jonas issued several intemperate press releases charging the committee with a partisan whitewash. Later he apologized. At issue here is whether Jonas knew that the Nye committee was authorized only to investigate excessive expenditures and not fraudulent voting practices.

MARCH 24, 1932

The Senate is debating H. R. 6662, proposing changes in the Tariff Act of 1930. Sen. Pat Harrison (D-Miss.) proposes amendments giving more power to Congress in fixing tariff rates and consenting to reciprocal trade agreements.

First subcommittee meeting—only Bankhead Thomas & I.[1] Bankhead's bill. I have more respect for Thomas than before. He knows the game and really wants to help.

Sen. Harrison talking on Tariff.

Blaine, Borah, Robinson etc. are exercised over something in a paper.[2] I'd like to see what it is. Of course I should not have so much curiosity. Pat made a facetious fair speech. Its over. Jno Abbott came and we went to lunch. I went over to the House. Saw all the Rep. from Ark. but Mr. Driver.[3]

Mr. and Mrs. Trout[4] came up from Jonesboro. I did enjoy seeing them. Both very friendly. He wanted to know, as friend, if I were to be a candidate. I was non committal.

1. Agriculture Subcommittee meeting with Sen. John Bankhead (D-Ala.) and Sen. John Thomas (R-Idaho).

2. Sen. John J. Blaine (R-Wisc.), Sen. William E. Borah (R-Idaho), and Sen. Arthur R. Robinson (R-Ind.); the "something in a paper" is not further identified.

3. Rep. William J. Driver (D-Ark.).

4. Mr. and Mrs. W. O. Troutt of Jonesboro. Mr. Troutt at the time was editor of the *Jonesboro Sun.*

MARCH 25, 1932

I did not know Senate had recessed until Monday so I came down. Had talk with Mr. Derrio[1] and his wife. Also a Union Labor man urging me to get into Senate race. Had talk with Paul Yates.[2] He was nice. Broke Bob's heart by leaving him to come home on car. We stopped by Sears & Roebucks.

1. Not identified.

2. See journal entry of March 1, 1932, n. 3.

MARCH 26 — 27, 1932

Stayed at home sweeping, dusting and making candy.

MARCH 28, 1932

Another day's debate on proposed amendments to the Tariff Act with Sen. Arthur H. Vandenberg (R-Mich.) defending high tariffs as essential mechanisms against further economic decline.

Ordered photographs. Came early. Stayed in Senate. Much discussion of Tariff headed by Vandenberg, who said those Democrats who oppose general Tariffs, but some special tariff for their States were "hitchhikers" and as such very dangerous.[1] Austin making maiden speech.[2] Long drawn out. Finally a move to Executive Session and Recess.

  1. Sen. Vandenberg, referring to Democrats who oppose tariffs generally but support protection for their constituents, notes that like hitchhikers, "They are liable to assault one before the ride is over; they are calculated to sue one for damages if an accident occurs; they contribute nothing to the journey but their own dead weight."
  2. Actually Sen. Warren R. Austin (R-Vt.) complies with so many requests to yield that he never gets to speak more than two sentences. It is the interruptions, rather than his speech, that are "long drawn out."

MARCH 29, 1932

The Senate is still debating the proposed Tariff Act amendments, and the remarks by Sen. Warren R. Austin (R-Vt.) in support of H. R. 6662 set off another round of biting partisan exchanges.

Austin in trouble in a colloquy. He will delve further into the facts before he starts his next speech, as on some phases he was not sufficiently informed to be able to answer.
Lovely luncheon today. Chicken a la king and cucumber onion

lettuce salad with Roquefort cheese dressing. Also lovely sunshine cake.

Mrs. Blaine[1] and I had cigarettes in my office. I believe the Republicans are howling for a Balanced Budget for political purposes.

1. Wife of Sen. John J. Blaine (R-Wisc.).

MARCH 30, 1932

The Senate continues discussing proposed tariff legislation with this day's debate dominated by Sen. Simeon D. Fess (R-Ohio).

My most difficult experience with an interviewer. I'm not giving out interviews. She made me out a communist—one utterly without taste, or anything else. I am disgusted.

Fess says his speeches are never revised. He has changed since he was in the House.

MARCH 31, 1932

Sen. Tom Connally (D-Tex.) and Sen. John Thomas (R-Idaho) join the debate on proposed tariff amendments.

Frances Pryor[1] came. So did Stasia.[2] Paul and Forrest came for lunch. I got a bad oyster. Had lunch. Ate at Vice President's table, I hadn't known it was his. Stasia & friend met the V.P. They met Huey Long, Lafollette and others. Said they were thrilled. Thomas talked. Connally made a good speech.

1. Daughter of Thomas B. Pryor, prominent attorney and Democratic party official from Fort Smith, Arkansas.
2. See journal entry for February 1, 1932, n. 1.

APRIL 1, 1932

After further discussion by Sen. Elmer Thomas (D-Okl.), Sen. Smith W. Brookhart (R-Iowa), and Sen. Henry D. Hatfield (D-

W.Va.), Sen Caraway joins a majority in adopting Sen. Pat Harrison's (D-Miss.) substitute tariff amendments.

Thomas talked & talked. Hatfield did no better. Then quorum call came. Pooh. They say we will vote between 3:30 & 4. Mr. Halsey[1] says only an optimist can say that. Now Brookhart is talking. We finally passed the Dem. substitute to the Tariff bill.

1. Edwin A. Halsey, secretary to the minority.

APRIL 2, 1932

Came down to Com. meeting—*no need.* Got home late worn out. Stasia[1] brought Bob home. She ate fried chicken with us last night.

1. See journal entry for February 1, 1932, n. 1.

APRIL 3, 1932

Worked in yard in white sunshine. Even tho it was Sunday. Forrest over for only an hour or so.

APRIL 4, 1932

A message from President Hoover suggesting that Congress make further cuts in his proposed budget prompts a lengthy speech by minority leader Joe Robinson accusing the president of shirking his budget-making responsibilities. Sen. Robinson also suggests deep cuts in government employees' salaries. His remarks prompt a furious speech by Sen. Huey Long, charging that salary cuts are mere sops and that the real need is for drastic corporate and inheritance taxes and a wholesale redistribution of wealth.

Read I was unanimously named to go as delegate to convention.[1] Many nice letters. Wrote numerous ones. Joe made a speech —saying cut all our salaries and get good moral effect from the country. Perhaps he is right.

Huey made a speech—much slinging of arms. Not so bad either. Just a bit radical. Probably serve a good purpose. Tho I'm a little afraid it may encourage radicalism.

Now we are discussing Jonas[2] again. We may hear as much about him as about Jonah who was swallowed by a whale.

1. Sen. Caraway was one of eight delegates at large named, along with six regular delegates, by the Democratic State Committee to represent Arkansas at the upcoming Democratic National Convention in Chicago.
2. See journal entry for March 23, 1932, n. 2. Sen. Daniel O. Hastings (R-Del.) moves that the Senate's rejection of Charles Jonas' nomination be reconsidered. His request is debated at length, then postponed.

APRIL 5, 1932

The nomination of Charles Jonas is reconsidered and again rejected; and Senate ratification of commercial trade treaties with Norway and Poland prompts a lengthy dialogue on the effects of such treaties on proposed tariff revisions. Sen. Kenneth McKellar (D-Tenn.) concludes the day by charging the Shipping Board with assorted acts of favoritism.

Met as usual. Everyone cheerful because the sun shines. Told Huey he owes me another silver cup for listening to his speech again. He says he will vote with me again sometime. Mrs. Keating and Mrs. Herrick[1] want me to talk and eat on May 2nd. Guess I won't. Listened to a lot of treaty talk today. May be very important—but most terribly uninteresting and especially when they talk so low you can't hear them.

Went to Senate Luncheon. Had Old Va. ham—grapefruit and avocado salad the cheese salad Mrs. Chonna[2] brought tasted like bed bugs smell. It was not good. Sat next Mrs. Vandenberg.[3] She is very nice. Really enjoyed it all. Wore my swearing dress.[4] Had nice talk with Mrs. Oddie about Mrs. Phipps.[5] Everything nice. Came back and voted against Jonas again. Seemed to be right to me. Mr. Reed voted with us—Borah Aye—Norbeck also Aye. Both of those surprised me.[6] McKellar talking again. Really he should let someone else talk some.

1. Mrs. Keating is probably Margaret, wife of Edward Keating, editor of *Labor*; Mrs. Herrick not identified.

2. Not identified.

3. Wife of Sen. Arthur Vandenberg (R-Mich.).

4. Dress worn for oath-taking ceremony, February 1, 1932.

5. Wife of Sen. Tasker L. Oddie (R-Nev.); discussing wife of former Sen. Lawrence C. Phipps (R-Cal.).

6. Sen. David A. Reed (R-Pa.) makes clear that he personally supports Jonas but hesitates to dishonor the unwritten rule of senatorial courtesy. Sen. William E. Borah (R-Idaho) and Sen. Peter Norbeck (R-N. Dak.), although nominally Republicans, rarely vote with their party; hence Sen. Caraway's surprise at their support for Jonas.

APRIL 6, 1932

Sen. Pat Harrison (D-Miss.) and Sen. James F. Byrnes (D-S.C.) join the Democratic chorus of protests against President Hoover's insistence that Congress is responsible for excessive spending and therefore should be responsible for budget cuts. Nothing is resolved, but the meandering dialogue prompts an equally meandering poem.

Not much. Many speeches. Pat a good one. Burns a short one. I had some callers who were very nice. Father Hegeman[1] of Little Rock. All day much talk.

Criticising Mr. Hoover seems the order of the day
And'i'faith I am much with them.
All our horses need more Hay.
But to combine Bureaus many
Is opposed on every hand.
"Soak the rich" to the last penny—
Balanced Budget the demand.

If 'twere balanced now tomorrow
Would our plight less direful be?
In our land there's so much sorrow
Would this temporary be?

Something's wrong — and very rotten
Where we're heading, can you see?
The Republicans have forgotten
They're to bring prosperity.

If we only had a glass of beer
To wet our throats, why then
We would perforce have a simulated cheer
Could cure the wants of men.

To cater to the apetites. But never make men drunk
In competition with lawless wets
to whose level we have sunk.

If from our woes, and they are many
We pass this bill to save us.
Why ne'er a grain of sense have any
The votes that way belave us.

To train my boys to make of them
Men of honesty wealth and brain
I strove the wilder traits to stem
Nor heeding their pleadings vain.

To give them always their own way
was no curb, nor way to control
Avoid evil appearance — take the right way
Is the way to reach the goal
Of man's stature with wealth and mind intact,
Connive not with wrong to reach your end
In governments — in life, in fact.

1. Not identified.

APRIL 7, 1932

Sen. Caraway seems to have enjoyed her first Democratic caucus, during which Sen. Cameron Morrison (D-S.C.) apparently protested the "soak-the-rich" tax sentiments of some of his more liberal colleagues. The major item of Senate business is S. J. Res. 131, appropriating $5 million for the relief of certain storm-stricken states. Sen. Caraway supported this measure

when it was unanimously reported by the Agriculture Com-
mittee but now is impressed with Sen. Marvel Logan's (D-Ky.)
speech against the federal government's bailing out the states.

1st Caucus. It was great. Demagogery rampant. What is to
come. No care whither coffee tariff or not—but—must get into
record they want it. Cam Morrison against soaking the taxes on
the rich. It is funny to watch them squirm. Perhaps if I had 16
millions I wouldn't want to have my taxes raised either.
Mr. Logan made a good speech. I'm glad I did not miss it. He
was against so much help to the States. He was really good. I
wanted to vote with him—but because I had voted for the bill in
the Com. I couldn't do that.

APRIL 8, 1932

Quorum calls indicate Sen. Caraway was present throughout
a long day's discussion of tariffs and appropriations. No votes
were taken.

Margot[1] to come tonight. She's sweet. Much talk. Not much
doing—awfully tired.

1. Margot Willis, Forrest's friend from Port Washington, N.Y.

APRIL 9, 1932

Mal—Paul—Forrest—Mr. Davis—Miss Fyfield—Miss Bailess—
Ruth Hughes—Margot—Auntie, Bob and I all for dinner.[1] I had
chicken dressing candied s. potatoes—green peas—grapefruit &
avocado salad—strawberry short cake—soup Melba Toast—
coffee. Celery salted nuts, biscuit all for one dinner. Bertha served.[2]

1. A number of Forrest's friends joined the family for dinner: Malcolm Price,
Rita Baylis, Ruth Hughes (daughter of Rep. William Hughes [D-N.J.]), and Margot
Willis, Forrest's friend. Others not identified.
2. Housekeeper.

APRIL 10, 1932

Margot[1] left. Forrest slept all day.

1. Margot Willis, Forrest's friend.

APRIL 11, 1932

While the Senate disposes of numerous minor bills on the calendar, Sen. Caraway reports on visitors, constituent correspondence, and a partisan exchange.

Tired to death. Met Mrs. Couch[1] for first time. She & Johnson[2] in Gallery. Very nice. Mrs. Nicholson came up with her cousin. Mrs. Roach asked me to lunch, a Mrs. McGuire from N.Y. with her.[3]

I got a letter from printing agency in little Rock—sent airmail unstamped—cost me 4 cts.—and he was protesting against raising postage rates to 3 cts for letter. I suggested Garrett write him I couldn't see where the raise would affect him as he seemed to let the other fellows pay it.

I told Watson[4] yesterday, "What is your Pres. going to do now since his fish got into the wrong stream." He said "I'll tell him there are still a lot of suckers" then I—"Yes and it begins to look he's going to catch 'em again, I'm sorry to say." Then a loud guffaw.

1. Wife of Harvey C. Couch; see journal entry for January 11, 1932, n. 2.
2. One of the Couch's four sons.
3. Wife of Rep. William N. Roach (D-N.Y.) with unidentified friend.
4. Sen. James E. Watson (R-Ind.).

APRIL 12, 1932

The Senate continues debate on Interior Department appropriations; Sen. Caraway seems more interested in the menu of the Congressional Club lunch.

Many letters—not greatly personal. Debate on Interior Appropriations.

Went to Luncheon. Furnished coffee. Had Tongue—Ham—dill pickles—avocado salad—grapefruit—and waldorf salad—sunshine, angel and chocolate cake—I overate.

Stayed on floor most of afternoon. Went home very tired.

Long distance call from Gov. about Decker Bush[1] of Texarkana for Federal Judge—made no promise.

1. Circuit Judge Dexter Bush of Prescott, Arkansas, did not become a federal judge.

APRIL 13, 1932

During continued Senate debate on Interior Department appropriations, Sen. Tom Connally (D-Tex.) protests the Interior Secretary's announcement to open all public lands for oil exploration; Sen. Arthur Robinson (R-Ind.) interrupts Sen. Park Trammell's (D-Fla.) speech opposing additional funds for Howard University with an allegation of Democratic campaign spending irregularities; and Sen. Huey Long (D-La.) enters each of these debates with his usual antiwealth sentiments.

Early to work. Talked to Sen. Dill about the subcommittee.[1] Nice letter from Sharp Dunnaway.[2] Connally a good speech. Robinson a rabid partisan speech injected into Trammel's speech. He is at it again. Huey has sat in Joe's seat nearly all day. Neeley[3] says Joe will do well if Huey lets him stay in Senate another term. That he is most eager person to burst into limelight on all occasions of anyone he ever saw. He's right on every count—but didn't ask me to concur.

I'm not a good enough sport to enjoy hearing Robinson cuss the "dimmicrats." Long is certainly cussing the Republicans now. I'm not enjoying that much either.

1. Discussion with Sen. Clarence C. Dill (D-Wash.) regarding an unidentified subcommittee. Dill chaired the Senate Interstate Commerce Committee.
2. L. S. Sharpe Dunaway, long-time traveling representative for the *Arkansas Gazette.* For his later interpretation of Sen. Caraway's 1932 campaign, see William C. Mears, "L. S. (Sharpe) Dunaway," *Arkansas Historical Quarterly* 13 (1954).
3. Sen. Matthew M. Neely (D-W. Va.).

APRIL 14, 1932

The Senate is debating another of Sen. Kenneth McKellar's (D-Tenn.) motions to cut appropriations by 10 percent, this time from the Treasury and Post Office departments. Sen. Henry F. Ashurst (D-Ariz.) argues that cutting building funds would only increase unemployment.

"The man who in the peril of country keeps his temper is a moral coward." Ashurst to McKellar in discussion of Judiciary appropriation Bill. Met Raskob—Shouse—Mr. Rose and others at luncheon in Joe's room in Capitol.[1] I did not enjoy it much. Sprained my ankle—very painful—Stayed home all day Friday the 15th. Spent Sat. at home resting my foot. Mrs. Sigman and Mrs. Weinmann[2] came out for dinner on Sunday. Used best china. Soup lamb roast mint jelly—Tomato aspic with cucumbers onions hard boiled eggs Roquefort cheese balls—upside down cake—Homemade candy—Mrs. Nicholson and Mrs. Butler[3] from Nashville came out. Very good day.

1. John J. Raskob of New York City, controversial chairman of the Democratic National Committee; Joe H. Shouse of Alabama, chairman of the Executive Committee of the National Democratic party; and D. Kenneth Rose, national executive secretary of the Democratic Victory Campaign.
2. Mrs. Martin L. Sigman of Monticello and Mrs. John F. Weinmann of Little Rock, both prominent in the Daughters of the American Revolution and in Arkansas Democratic circles.
3. Mrs. William J. Nicholson with unidentified friend.

APRIL 18, 1932

Sen. Daniel O. Hastings (R-Del.) had apparently arranged for a pair with Sen. Caraway, and since the Senate is voting on a number of miscellaneous items, she is required to speak out for the first time.

Early in my chair. Had to announce my pair—3 times—It was nerve racking but I will be heard. Anyway one other bridge crossed. Hartsill surprised us by changing his mind again.[1] I'm just quiescent. Put Mrs. Wingo—Otis and some friends in gallery.[2] Mrs. Roberts (Emily came down for a few moments).[3]

1. Rep. Heartsill Ragon (D-Ark.) was so widely considered to be a certain contender for the Senate that his announcement that he would run for reelection to the House caused general surprise.

2. Rep. Effiegene Wingo (D-Ark.) who was elected on November 4, 1930, to take her deceased husband's place in the House until his term expired in March 1931, was simultaneously elected to the ensuing term and served until March 4, 1933; here with her son, Otis Theodore Wingo, Jr.

3. Not identified.

APRIL 19, 1932

The Senate is still dealing with miscellaneous appropriations items, and Sen. Caraway is still paired with the absent Sen. Hastings. The Senate adjourns early in respect for their colleague, Sen. William J. Harris (D-Ga.), who had died the previous day.

Today so very like yesterday. Except they announced Sen. Harris death and funeral arrangements. I couldn't go to the luncheon I was so upset. Had to announce my pair again several times. Sen. Costigan[1] very kindly told me I had a very good speaking voice—clear, soft, and easily understood. That was nice of him. I wrote a poem on beer. A la Tydings.[2]

1. Sen. Edward P. Costigan (D-Colo.).

2. Sen. Millard E. Tydings (D-Md.), one of the most vocal advocates of repealing prohibition, read into the *Congressional Record* a lengthy argument for repeal prepared by the Women's Organization for National Prohibition Reform. Sen. Caraway's "beer" poem has not been preserved.

APRIL 20, 1932

Because of Sen. William J. Harris' death, the Senate is in recess; and Sen. Caraway uses the day for shopping.

Went down to Garfinckels with Mrs. Harrison.[1] Bought two silk dresses—a sweater suit & blouse—a hat—and ordered 3 cotton

dresses — black dotted swiss. We had lunch at Peoples. I bought
some stockings and handkerchiefs — and magazines. Then home.
Sen. Harris funeral was why I did not come.

1. Wife of Sen. Pat Harrison (D-Miss.).

APRIL 21, 1932

*The Senate has begun discussing the Alabama senatorial con-
test between John H. Bankhead and Thomas J. Heflin. Former
Sen. Heflin, who had been a close friend of Thad Caraway,
bolted the Democratic party in 1928 in protest against Democratic nominee Al Smith's Catholicism and managed Herbert
Hoover's presidential campaign in Alabama. The Democratic
party retaliated by refusing Heflin permission to run in the
Democratic primary in 1930. John Bankhead won the primary,
and although Heflin then filed as an Independent, he was
beaten by Bankhead in the general election. Heflin has challenged both the legality of the Alabama Democratic party's
action barring him from the primary and the integrity of the
general election process. The Senate Committee on Privileges
and Elections has concluded its investigation and declared
Bankhead the duly elected senator from Alabama, but their
report must now be accepted by the full Senate.*

On hand. Huey back. The Bankhead resolution to come up
today. J. T. Johnson[1] came and called me out. He looks so like his
father.

How may one disconcert an argument. Sen. Black arose and
asked Sen. Bratton if it would disconcert his argument any to
read some argument in some case in the House.[2] Got my pictures
from U. & U.[3] Some very good. Went home on st. car. Missed my
train.

1. A West Memphis, Arkansas, car dealer active in Crittenden County politics.
2. Sen. Hugo Black (D-Ala.) asks Sen. Sam G. Bratton (D-N.Mex.), "Would it disconcert the Senator's argument to have inserted in the Record at this place a few
lines from a decision in the House of Representatives on the law of the case?"

3. Photographs from Underwood and Underwood, a prominent Washington, D.C., photographic studio.

APRIL 22, 1932

The Senate is still debating the Bankhead-Heflin election contest.

Arrived early. Looked at the mail. Went down to Garfinckels. Bought coat, wool dress, and had net sleeved dress fitted. W&L[1] — Bought some compotes — clear & green glass plates — blue oatmeal dishes — and a casserole.

Yesterday while I was solving a cross word puzzle[2] Sen. Tydings[3] passed and said "The name of a river in Siberia" — I said "What is the name of best drink in the world?" He grinned and said "water". I said, "No, No, Your answer would surely be *beer.*"

Some big stick was sent to Robinson, Ind. to use on Sons of Wild Jack Asses — so inscribed on the club. He very gracefully presented it to the author of the now famous phrase.[4]

1. Woodward and Lothrop, a Washington department store.
2. No doubt to the consternation of her colleagues, Sen. Caraway occasionally worked crossword puzzles while seated at her desk in the Senate. When asked about this pastime in a postelection press conference, she replied: "It is true I occasionally worked crossword puzzles, but I heard so many cross words there that the puzzles became so easy they were uninteresting." *Arkansas Gazette,* August 17, 1932.
3. Sen. Millard Tydings (D-Md.), champion of repeal.
4. Actually the Galesburg, North Dakota, Farmers Union Local sent this club cut from a cottonwood tree not to Sen. Arthur R. Robinson (R-Ind.) but to Sen. Gerald P. Nye (R-N. Dak.), who in turn presented it to Sen. George Moses (R-N.H.). See journal entry for December 15, 1931, n. 7.

APRIL 23, 1932

The Bankhead-Heflin contest is still being debated. Sen. Hugo Black, senior senator from Alabama, is managing the pro-Bankhead forces, with suggestions from Bankhead himself.

Had a call from Mr. Holmes.[1] We agree on a good many things. He seems strong on Heflin. I can't vote for Tom though.

Black now speaking for Bankhead. He is trying to be very repressed and very lawyer like. Some are staying — many going and coming. I'm catching up on my journal but seeing a good many things — and hearing Mr. B. prompt him.

1. George Sanford Holmes, Washington correspondent for the *Birmingham Post* and other newspapers.

APRIL 25, 1932

The Senate is still discussing the Bankhead-Heflin contest, with today's debate revolving around a motion by Sen. Park Trammell (D-Fla.) that Heflin be permitted to address the Senate in his own behalf. Sen. Joseph T. Robinson (D-Ark.) and Sen. Charles L. McNary (R-Ore.) argue against the Trammell motion, but it carries thirty-three to thirty-one, with Sen. Caraway joining the minority opposing it.

After a hectic trip home on stcar on Saturday — and a visit from Mrs. Sigman[1] thru Sunday, and not much rest on Sun. night I found myself moved up in the Senate and I'm not much crazy about it.[2] They're discussing Bankhead again. He (Tom) and Bankhead are sitting near to each. They're like two cats on a shed.

Robinson holds that Heflin has no right to speak on the contest because the question is not that Heflin was elected. Instead the question is that there was no election in the State of Alabama.[3] It is a sad affair. I really feel that Tom has no right to speak. In fact I do not think he should have brought such contumely on his state. I think he was lacking in State pride and personal dignity. He was crazy on one subject and disgraced himself by voting for Hoover. For the reason of Al Smith's religion.

I like for the underdog to be heard — but I'm hopeful Tom won't make a speech. Guess I'm not big enough or broad enough to be a politician. Trammel is so weak and so puerile. I wish he had got done. "A bad precedent never makes a good practice" — Sen. McNary in regard to Tom being allowed to speak.[4]

1. See journal entry for April 14, 1932, n. 2.

2. Sen. William J. Harris' death has moved Sen. Caraway up one notch in seniority and changed the seating on the Senate floor. She is still next to Sen. Huey Long but no longer within easy chatting distance of Sen. Marvel Logan.

3. Sen. Robinson's argument is that since the matter officially before the Senate is the Election Committee's recommendation that Bankhead be seated and that even if the report is rejected Heflin would still not be entitled to take the seat, Heflin has no more right to address the Senate than any other member of the Alabama electorate.

4. Sen. McNary argues that no matter how many similar precedents Sen. Trammell may cite of nonsenators addressing the Senate, "a bad precedent never makes a good practice."

APRIL 26, 1932

Former Sen. Thomas Heflin speaks over five hours in his own defense, invoking the Bible, court records, the testimony of friends and supporters, and countless folksy aphorisms. He frequently elicits laughter and manages to fling a great deal of mud on Sen. John Bankhead, but he does not persuade Sen. Caraway to his cause.

Heflin speaking "The devil can quote scripture for his purpose."[1] Smith drew immense crowds too, but he seemed to fail in the count too.[2] The false note struck when he claims he would have been killed had his friends not given notice goodby to Bankhead too.[3] He reached great heights of oratory but got so high he had much trouble alighting. He talked for 1 hr. & 45 min. then said he could not finish in two hours. So Mr. Norris[4] moved that he have unanimous consent to conclude. It was given, so he talked until 5:10. Told all he knew two or three times. Really think he hurt himself. Of course he was fighting for his life and I could see the pathos—and be sorry. However I feel most strongly that it was unfair to his state to contest under the circumstances. He bolted the national ticket—and to me he was legally barred from becoming a candidate in the primaries.

1. This is Sen. Caraway's response to Heflin's frequent quoting of scripture, beginning with, "Know the truth and the truth shall make you free," and ending with, "The time shall come when a man's foes shall be those of his own household."

2. Apparently a reference to Al Smith, 1928 Democratic presidential nominee, who — like Heflin — attracted enormous crowds but lost the election.

3. Heflin speaks frequently of death knells, political assassination, and political murder but does not ever imply that his life was threatened. "Goodby to Bankhead too" apparently refers to Heflin's frequent charge that Bankhead was personally aware of and involved in the assorted corruptions Heflin alleges.

4. Sen. George W. Norris (R-Neb.) bolted his party to support Al Smith in 1928; hence his sympathy for Heflin.

APRIL 27, 1932

The Bankhead-Heflin question continues: Sen. Bankhead finally speaks in his own defense, following the long string of charges by former Sen. Heflin. Sen. George W. Norris (R-Neb.), interrupted by Sen. Daniel O. Hastings (R-Del.), argues that the Alabama primary was unconstitutional and therefore Heflin's claims are valid.

The contest still at white heat. Sen. Bankhead made a long speech. I heard most of it. Norris made a speech and Hastings. We stayed down until nearly 7 waiting for Mrs. Sigman.[1] She spent night. Saw O. K. Halladay.[2]

The new Sen. Cohen[3] sworn, a big luncheon by Ga. delegation — "The King is dead long live the king.".

1. See journal entry for April 14, 1932, n. 2.
2. Not identified.
3. Sen. John S. Cohen (D-Ga.), appointed by Gov. Richard B. Russell to fill the vacancy created by Sen. William J. Harris' death.

APRIL 28, 1932

After another day-long debate, Sen. John Bankhead is pro-nounced, by a sixty-four to eighteen vote, the duly elected senator from Alabama. Sen. Caraway votes with the majority but obviously feels some compassion for former Sen. Heflin.

Had a hectic time getting Mrs. Humphrey[1] and others in to lunch. Auntie & Judge Halladay[2] came late. We finally voted on

Heflin-Bankhead. The vote was a vindication of Alabama and her elections at least I so see it. Did feel terribly, to see Tom go out rather broken. It is hard to vote to take a man's whole life in a way. Mrs. Sigman[3] left at 6:50. It was so nice to see someone I knew and could talk to, nice too to rest some more. Most interesting meeting of the Agriculture Com. The ladies seemed to enjoy it.

1. Possibly the wife of Arkansas state auditor, J. Oscar Humphrey.
2. Not identified.
3. See journal entry for April 14, 1932, n. 2. Martin L. Sigman, a cotton ginner, was in Washington to testify on proposed cotton legislation before the Senate Agriculture Committee.

APRIL 29, 1932

Sen. Caraway spends the day in committee meetings and misses a sharp exchange between Sen. Joe Robinson and Sen. Huey Long over the latter's proposal to prohibit, through tax reform, anyone earning over $1 million annually or inheriting more than $5 million.

Meeting of Agriculture Committee both morning and afternoon. Huey and Joe locked horns. I did not hear it but it made good reading. Baldy Jackson[1] came to see me. I said nothing.

1. W. D. Jackson, Little Rock labor leader, active in Democratic politics.

APRIL 30, 1932

The Senate debates and adds numerous perfecting amendments to appropriations bills for the State, Justice, Labor and Commerce departments.

Came down. There was no vote of importance. Had a political talk with Joe. He said some nice things. I'm still up in the air. Went to dinner at Washington Country Club. Lovely lobster dinner. I am unwilling to go with certain people or sorts of people. I do not like voices and words inspired by rye.

Forrest and friend and Mal[1] home for supper. They seemed to have a good time.

Sunday as usual. Auntie came late. Spent the night. Told of nice house on 2nd St. Moderate rent.

1. Malcolm Price, a friend of Forrest.

MAY 2, 1932

Sen. Caraway makes no comment on the official business of the Senate—the naval building program—but comments instead on former Rep. Jeanette Rankin, utility magnate Harvey Couch, and the ongoing feud between Sen. Joe Robinson and Sen. Huey Long.

Got down early. Forrest came in. I'm so sorry I had engagement and couldn't have him for lunch. Miss Rankin,[1] 1st woman Congressman came in. I'm not strong for her. Not any sort of jealousy the cause either. I do not like her manner. I do not like her reputation etc. etc.

Am wearing a new dress because am to have lunch with Mr. Couch and some of his female relatives—Mrs. Pete Couch (Shreveport La.) Mrs. Monroe, sister, Magnolia Ark.—Mrs. Armstrong—his sister from California.[2] They insisted so I told him the Hoovers were, personally, very unpopular.

I did not attend the dinner Mr. Couch gave at the Mayflower that night in their honor. Huey was saying Joe was a fool—that he (Huey) was no leader—he was the Kingfish. I asked him which he thought was most descriptive, King or fish? He laughed—but I thought for a while he had been offended.

1. Jeanette Rankin (R-Mont.) was elected to Congress in 1916, four years before national women's suffrage. At this time, having been defeated in a bid for the Senate in 1918, she was legislative secretary of the National Council for the Prevention of War, lobbying for a policy of strict neutrality. She was an outspoken crusader for her causes: women's suffrage, tax reform, maternal and child welfare, and, especially, pacifism. Which of these causes, or her vigorous manner of pursuing them, inspired Sen. Caraway's distaste is not clear.

2. For Harvey Couch, see journal entry for January 11, 1932, n. 2; here with the wife of his brother and chief associate, Charles Peter ("Pete") Couch of Shreveport; and with his two sisters, Mrs. George B. Monroe of Magnolia, Arkansas, and Mrs. Armstrong of California.

MAY 3, 1932

The Senate has become increasingly embroiled in Sen. Long's daily attacks on Sen. Robinson. The preceding day, with great fanfare, Long resigned from all committees in symbolic rejection of Robinson's party leadership. On this day he reads into the Congressional Record *a list of the "power interests" represented by Robinson's Little Rock law firm.*

Senate luncheon. I was placed on Commerce Committee.[1] Huey says Joe doesn't look really as well with his hair died. When he says things like that you have to laugh—but I told him he surely wouldn't make me go on record on *that*. Had visit from Mr. Jackson—read him my "red boot" poem.[2] It is good, but I cry every time I read it. Heartsill has announced for his same Congress seat.[3] Huey had read a list of corporations etc. which Joe's legal firm represent.[4] I'm afraid Joe is on his last leg politically, unless he gets a judgeship or a cabinet place.

Guess my political life is nearly over, as well as my physical one. It saddens one to think of the years and years of dependence one may have to endure.

1. Sen. Caraway received Sen. Long's vacated seat on the Commerce Committee.
2. "Baldy" Jackson (see journal entry for April 29, 1932, n. 1). The poem has not been preserved.
3. Rep. Ragon's announced explanation for seeking reelection to the House, rather than making the anticipated Senate race, was that the country's dire economic circumstances required constant attention, and he dared not take the time from official duties for a time-consuming primary race. Within one year's time, he was named a federal judge.
4. The list includes the Arkansas, Louisiana, Mississippi, and Southern Power and Light Companies, various banks, phone companies, insurance companies, and building and loan associations.

MAY 5, 1932

*Sen. Caraway had sent out a number of letters to test the
political waters and comments here on the discouraging—
but apparently not definitive—response.*

Some letters came without offering a great deal of consolation.
I'm so afraid my judgment is so warped by my desires in the
matter that I can not come happily to any decision. I have had to
be so alone, so very close mouthed that mayhap my chances are
not so good. I know I've had no offers of help from any political
leader.

Had luncheon with Sen. Kean.[1] Met Archie Roosevelt.[2] Mrs.
Stubblefield[3] came in. Saw Mr. Jackson[4] and his friends. Dan and
Mrs. S. came in.[5] Nothing yet decided.

1. Sen. Hamilton F. Kean (R-N.J.).
2. Son of President Theodore Roosevelt.
3. See journal entry for February 27, 1932, n. 1.
4. Ibid., April 29, 1932, n 1.
5. Probably Forrest's friend Dan Fahey, with Hattie's friend, Mrs. Stubblefield.

MAY 6, 1932

*The Senate is considering a controversial expansion of the
naval building program, which Sen. Caraway votes to support.
She is obviously preoccupied, however, with the upcoming
deadline for entering the Democratic primary in Arkansas.*

At office early. Letters just as usual. At last a letter from those
I sent out. Just a resume of the situation. What a momentous
decision. "To be or not to be"—consistency, or constancy or
something "Thou art not a woman."

After Monday I'll either be much keyed up or on my way to the
simple life, maybe. We vote today and won't come back. We did
adjourn until Monday.

MAY 7, 1932

I am a nervous wreck. Stayed in bed and read "Marion Grey" by Mary J. Holmes. How in the world I ever adored her books so when I was a child. Maybe because they are *clean*. So few books are now.

Auntie came out late. I showed her my new clothes and we played "Double Canfield" — I won — she says with Bob's help.

MAY 9, 1932

A momentous day for Sen. Caraway: she becomes the first woman to preside over the Senate, and she commits herself to a race for reelection by sending her filing fee and party loyalty pledge to the state Democratic party.

Paul back from N.Y. We came down late. Garrett had been out of town. No letters of any note. My replies are not too good. Had a talk with Joe and Heartsill.[1] What their real thoughts are no one knows. They are as much up in the air as I am. Made history. Presided over the Senate while Mr. Glass[2] was speaking. It was snap judgement and I was scared. Nothing came up but oh, the autographs I signed. Well, I pitched a coin and heads came three times,[3] so because the boys wish, and because I really want to try out my own theory of a woman running for office I let my check and pledges be filed. And now won't be able to sleep or eat.

1. Sen. Joe Robinson and Rep. Heartsill Ragon.
2. Sen. Carter Glass (D-Va.).
3. The reference to pitching a coin is neither purely symbolic nor entirely accurate. According to Hattie's son Paul, he arrived in his mother's office to find her swinging slowly back and forth in the enormous official chair (her feet did not touch the ground) behind the equally enormous official Senate desk (which engulfed her.) She was expressing indecision about entering the Senate race, and Paul finally suggested tossing a coin. She agreed, suggesting heads she would run, tails she would not. Paul tossed, and the coin turned up tails, but she quickly interjected, "two out of three." The next two tosses brought heads, for which she was clearly hoping.

Hattie Caraway presiding over the Senate, May 9, 1932. New York Times Pictures.

MAY 10, 1932

The reality of the forthcoming contest is beginning to loom, and although several offer encouragement, Sen. Caraway realizes that she herself must "get busy."

After much indigestion and little sleep I am still gasping for breath after jumping off the "deep end." The water seems very chilly and I can not swim a single stroke. However, I can dig in and kick and keep afloat—and by pushing with my toes I often make it across the pool. If possible, I shall strangle and choke and cross this pool, with my courage intact—and come up still loving human kind regardless of the outcome. I will not deny that I would sleep better and enjoy my food more if I had not plunged.

Had pictures made with the gavel.[1] I still think that was not so good. Forrest—Train—and Capt. Jones[2] came to lunch. That kid ordered a $1.15 steak. The lunch cost me $3.95 & .40 tips making $4.35. I can't stand that often.

Dear, dear. I hope I live thru all this. Mr. Bankhead, Mr. Wheeler, Mr. Cohen[3] all say they hope I win. Mrs. Robinson[4] was very nice. Guess I must get my thinking cap on—and get busy. Evening Star wants me to talk over a nationwide hookup. I wonder—must not stop to wonder, but must work.

1. The gavel used when Sen. Caraway presided over the Senate the preceding day.
2. Forrest's friend William Train with an unidentified Capt. Jones.
3. Sen. John H. Bankhead (D-Ala.), Sen. Burton K. Wheeler (D-Mont.) and Sen. John S. Cohen (D-Ga.).
4. Probably the wife of Sen. Joseph T. Robinson.

MAY 11, 1932

The Senate is debating a bill by Sen. Carter Glass (D-Va.) to reform the federal reserve system. Sen. Caraway seems to have regained her composure and decided to enjoy the experience of running regardless of the outcome.

The pictures came out in N.Y. Times and Herald.[1] Wonderful? O, no! Just makes me feel sort of cheap. Thank God (in all reverence) that I am able to eat and sleep and laugh at myself. If I can hold on to my sense of humor and a modicum of dignity I shall have had a wonderful time running for office, whether I get there or not.

> To run and run and never fret
> Is worth it tho you may not get
> The breaks you wanted, nor the place
> You still may live by God's good grace.
> And when your life and work are done
> Find tho' you lost — you also won.

From the "Jingles of a Jennet, Written in the Senate."

Mr. Kean, talking on the Glass bill, tells a lovely bedtime story about some London banker wanting Bliss — and then taking Morgan, J.P. and starting on his short broad road to wealth.[2]

1. See illustration.
2. During debate on the Glass-Steagall bill, Sen. Hamilton F. Kean (R-N.H.), a banker, answers a question by Sen. John J. Blaine (R-Wisc.) with some historical background on the so-called House of Morgan, originated when a Mr. Peabody of London was referred by George Bliss, a dry goods merchant in Hartford, Conn., to Mr. Junius Morgan, another Hartford merchant, as a prospective business partner.

MAY 12, 1932

The Senate continues to debate proposed changes in the federal reserve system.

I am positively in a daze after hearing those discussions in the Agriculture Committee. It is parlous times, and the criticism which come to the people here makes my blood boil, because tho they mean it not so much for me — but knowing it is my problem as that of all of us yet. No one can really tell just what to do, or what the effect will be. They can only study the problems and remedies from every side, and with the thought in mind "will it pass the Senate?" and if so — "Will the President sign it?" Very few of the critics have any remedy or workable suggestion — so you can see where we are.[1] Oh well, there's only courage and honesty, and tenacity, largely endurance demanded of us. I really have very great admiration for the time and real effort expended by these men. I'm working as hard, and trying to understand. If the people of my State continue me here, I shall not regret the long hours, nor the mental strain — just because it was the work he loved. My, I feel so alone — so bad indeed — but I shall hold on to my courage. Mr. Gibson and Dr. Warren[2] came to see me first having waited what must have seemed ages before coming to office, when I had told the boy to have them come to the office. Something will have to be done — but what? A newspaper woman wanted to know how it felt to preside over the Senate etc. I told her it was just another duty one has to perform in the Senate. Also, just between ourselves, I told her there was absolutely nothing to it. It was best behaved crowd of men you ever saw. They let Mr. Glass go on speaking without any interruption whatever.[3] Huey made another attack on Joe.[4] It was an epitome of bad taste — and bad psychology. Poor lamb, who so adores the plaudits of the multitude — is making a spectacle of himself of which he will be ashamed as he gains in years and wisdom — If — !

I hope Joe will not answer. It seems to be to ignore it will be the dignified and wise course to pursue.

1. See journal entry for December 19, 1931, n. 1. Sen. Caraway's comments aptly summarize the inability of farm leaders and sympathetic legislators to agree on legislation that would be both useful to the farmers and acceptable to President Hoover.

2. Possibly Ray Gibson, Little Rock attorney, and strong Parnell supporter; with, possibly, "Doc" Warren of Arkansas Power and Light.

3. See journal entry for May 9, 1932.

4. Sen. Long's verbal assaults on Joe Robinson have become so virulent that this day Long is temporarily forced to desist as having violated the Senate rule prohibiting imputing unworthy motives to a colleague. He regained the floor, however, and continued to denounce Robinson's ties to banking, securities, utilities, and insurance interests.

MAY 13, 1932

While the Senate debates tax reform, Sen. Caraway grows uneasy about the ominous silence from Arkansas in response to her announcement.

Much company today. Miss Baylis and her mother.[1] A Mrs.
Laker and her two sons[2] from Switzerland with them. A canadian
newspaper woman—Miss Fraser[3] here too. Saw Mrs. Thacker[4]
again. She is very nice in spite of the fact that she collaborated
with Means on his book "The Strange Death of President Harding."

The mails are really too stingy of approbation or objection to
my announcement. However, the die is cast—and all I can do is
sit tight and take whatever of abuse or praise comes from such a
blow to tradition. Really the way of the Politician is hard.

1. Forrest's friend Rita Baylis.
2. Not identified.
3. Not identified.
4. May Dixon Thacker.

MAY 14, 1932

While the Senate discusses tax legislation and farm relief,
Sen. Caraway's thoughts turn to her campaign and to the
Long-Robinson feud.

Went to Garfinckels and had some dresses fitted. Am now
getting myself organized. Had it out with Garrett as to statement.[1]
I had my way about it. At least so far so good. Some newspaper
people said it was O.K. Went home early as they adjourned early,
at least weren't going to take a vote. The finding of the dead
Lindberg Baby killed all of Huey's publicity.[2] I did not hear his
speech. Joe seems crestfallen. He isn't being treated quite fairly.

1. Actually no formal announcement appears in the Arkansas press until July,
when a series of statements stress that she is running for reelection on the basis
of her record: economy in government, and relief for those who need help. *Arkan-*
sas Gazette, July 15, 16, 20, 1932.
2. On the afternoon of May 12, the press announced that the Lindbergh baby
had been found dead.

MAY 15, 1932

Made candy—pulled weeds—read some Western thrillers.
Talked to Lillian[1] and Mrs. Doss.[2]

1. Dr. Lillian Malone, a psychiatrist, originally from Jonesboro, one of Sen. Caraway's closest friends.
2. Probably the wife of national labor leader A. S. Doss.

MAY 16, 1932

While the Senate debates proposed tax reform legislation, Sen. Caraway faces the increasingly unpleasant political realities.

One of the most interesting days in the Senate. Discussion of Couzens Amendment.[1] I voted aye. Night session. I didn't stay but was paired for the Connally Amendment.[2] My mail was heartbreaking. I'm in for crucifixion. I won't be the first woman who has been sacrificed to the ambition of some man. However I have no one but my own stubborness to blame. I found that the great gesture was only a gesture. To have preserved one's illusions this long is entirely to my credit I think. Woe! Woe! Woe! "Woe is me to have I've been to see what I see!"

The record was rather good reading. Huey told some rather funny stories. Seems to have talked 3 hrs.[3]

1. Sen. James Couzens (R-Mich.) proposes an amendment to tax reform legislation authorizing substantially steeper taxes on high-income brackets.
2. Sen. Tom Connally (D-Tex.) proposes an amendment authorizing more sharply progressive taxes than the Senate Finance Committee recommended but not as stiff as those advocated in the Couzens amendment.
3. Sen. Huey Long speaks for hours on the necessity of making the wealthy bear most of the tax burden.

MAY 17, 1932

During continued debate on tax reform, Sen. Caraway consistently votes with a liberal minority attempting to place the major burden on the wealthy, a position strongly opposed by Sen. Joe Robinson. She is opposed to, but amused by, Sen. Millard E. Tyding's (D-Md.) attempt to legalize 2.75 beer by taxing its ingredients.

Disappointed in the mail again. I almost weep and then I rave — no wonder my hair won't stay in wave. Have seen a good many people—all lobbyists. Mrs. Miller[1] did come and she is sweet.

I kept voting against Joe today. His Bro-in-law[2] seems to have got into trouble but they kept it out of papers here—and the Ark. papers but it got into Tenn papers. Seems to have got drunk and had a girl in his room and lost a diamond ring and the girl both— at once. But my brother got into limelight all right.[3] 10 min. to 8 P.M. Huey has talked—nearly everybody here has talked—and we are away down on the tax bill. Tydings, after much maneuvering, is now talking on beer, with his tongue in his cheek. It is the most ridiculous four-flushing I've ever seen—and I've laughed until I'm ashamed. He and Walsh[4] are working together so seriously it is the most really ludicrous thing I've ever seen—And how the galleries are eating it up. They are apparently very thirsty —the galleries I mean.

It is 8:30. I've telephoned Paul—and am going home soon. Sen. Smoot[5] very kindly surprised me by coming to me and telling me that they would not vote tonight. Very thoughtful and kind I thought.

1. Possibly the wife of Arkansas Rep. John E. Miller.
2. A reference to Grady Miller, Sen. Joseph T. Robinson's brother-in-law and employee. See journal entry for February 9, 1932, n. 1.
3. See ibid., February 18, 1932, n. 2.
4. Sen. David I. Walsh (D-Mass.).
5. Sen. Reed Smoot (R-Utah).

MAY 18, 1932

Sen. Caraway's amusement has turned to disgust with those senators—Millard Tydings (D-Md.), David I. Walsh (D-Mass.), Edwin S. Broussard (D-La.)—attempting to legalize 2.75 beer, and she joins a sixty-one to twenty-four majority rejecting their proposal. The Senate then takes up parts of the proposed tax bill imposing taxes on imported oil, which Sen. Caraway, unlike Sen. Robinson, supports.

In meeting at 11 A.M. Sen. Walsh now speaking on Tyding's amendment. When they talk on referendum of modification of Volstead Act, it is all Hooey. However, it softens their voices, and makes a rather pitiful appeal to please give 'em their beer. To see grown men act in such a manner—sophistry, and psychology and pretended humanitarianism is really a spectacle. Today I saw a decided resemblance between Joe and his nephew Joe Brewer.[1] I'm sorry Joe has fallen upon evil days.[2] He is really so attractive when he unbends—but naturally very peppery and arrogant. Mr. Broussard made a speech telling how legal Mr. Tydings beer will be. He was very very dry in his delivery to be so wet in his talk. Mr. Sheppard[3] talking. His speech is very very dry in every way.

Now, we come to the tariff parts and I am parting company with Joe on it.

I am still all in—both mentally and physically. Went home early—got a pair on the tariff on oil. I was pro. Paul had date. Bob & I alone—very lonely.

1. Sen. Joseph T. Robinson's nephew and staff member.
2. Sen. Robinson's "having fallen upon evil days" is simply Sen. Caraway's summation of the increased attacks, initiated by Sen. Long, but taken up by other critics, upon Robinson's corporate connections.
3. Sen. Morris Sheppard (D-Tex.).

MAY 19, 1932

The Senate's continued debate on proposed tariffs on imported oil as part of the tax bill prompts Sen. Caraway to articulate some aspects of her own political philosophy: suspicion of big business and protection of her state's economic interests.

Paul and I went to look at a house. It is brand new—small but pretty nice. We may take it. However, Paul & Garrett have gone to look at another home. It is too high priced, but we may take it.

Attended Com. on Commerce. Early to Senate. Tydings making speech against the tariff. Says he will soon finish the farmers, and I wanted to say he is already finished. He has quit using tractors and Fords, and going back to growing 15 ct corn, and cheap oats, to furnish horse power (Maryland is rightfully referred to as a little State, if judged by Dem. Senator)—rather than to buy gasoline.[1]

I am really against a tariff — any tariffs — but if New England is going to have protection for all her industries, I want our Ark. oils to have some protection.

I very foolishly tried to talk to Joe today. Never again. (Maybe if Rockefeller or Standard Oil had *seen* Mr. Tydings he would be on the other side.) He was cooler than a fresh cucumber and sourer than a pickled one.[2]

Mr. Hull[3] says we are under oath to represent all the people and here we are asked to grant a subsidy to the biggest business in this country except the banking business. The Moratorium was a subsidy to the banks, at least the same thing — and additional help to them by the Reconstruction Finance Corporation.

Got so sleepy, and not wanting to be heralded in the press as being sleeping on my job I got a pair and went to the office.

1. Sen. Millard E. Tydings (D-Md.) uses extensive data on gasoline consumption by farmers to argue against the proposed tariff on imported oil.

2. Sen. Caraway's relationship with Sen. Robinson has apparently further deteriorated, probably as a result of her persistent friendship with Sen. Long.

3. Sen. Cordell Hull (D-Tenn.).

MAY 20, 1932

After further extensive debate, the Senate adopts the oil tariff, forty-three to thirty-seven.

Still much talk. Night sessions. Finally a vote on the oil. I voted Aye — tho agonized over it. There's no straight and narrow way. You just have to rock along as best you can.

MAY 21, 1932

Huey called me offered to donate to my campaign and work for me. I can't sell my soul and live with myself. It would mean nothing to me to sit here day after day and have no freedom of voting.[1]

1. Discussed in the introduction.

MAY 22, 1932

First experience of meeting a beer drunk. He wanted to kiss my hand. I did not permit. I am not Royalty. Auntie came out and got mad because Bob tried to have fun at her expense.

MAY 23 — 28, 1932

The Senate devotes a full week of marathon sessions to amending the multisection tax reform bill.

All very much the same — night sessions until Thursday — Then meeting 10 A.M. to 7:30 P.M. Not much done.

MAY 30, 1932

Fifty-five senators, including Sen. Caraway, Sen. Long, and Sen. Robinson, in an effort to hasten final passage of the tax bill, released a statement that they would not vote for a general sales tax. This round-robin announcement is deplored all day long by other senators as stifling full discussion and debate.

Arrived at office 8:05. Not many political letters. Others pretty much.

Mr. Couch came in. No comfort.[1] Guess I'm a goat all right.

This has been most hectic day. Much talk. Finally remaining until 7:15 P.M. The sales Tax in discord. The vote to come at 10:30 A.M. Tues. morning. Packed and tried to do many things toward moving.

1. See journal entry for January 11, 1932, n. 2. Since Harvey Couch seems to have been one of those friends, and probably the most influential one, who assured Gov. Parnell that Hattie would not attempt to extend her term in the Senate, he must have been especially chagrined with her announcement and doubly unhappy with her growing friendship with Sen. Long, who daily attacked what he referred to as the power interests. It is not surprising that Couch gave Sen. Caraway "no comfort" during his visit.

MAY 31, 1932

The Senate has a final marathon session, with numerous roll-call votes, on the tax bill.

Just got in as they called my name. Hope there won't be so much wrangling today, and that I can get away. Stayed until 12 midnight & voted for the tax bill.

JUNE 1—2, 1932

While the Senate struggles with appropriations recommendations designed to balance the budget, Sen. Caraway takes two days off to settle into her new and more modest residence.

Stayed home and packed. Old man Pickford[1] came out. Hate him. Got into House 130 C St. S.E. after dark. Stayed night with Auntie. Bertha[2] came and we got house sort of in order. Came back to work on Friday June 3rd 1932. Mrs. Fullbright[3] came to see me. Lamar Williamson[4] and his children came. Will talk with him. No vote. Went home—a good night.

1. Not identified.
2. Housekeeper.
3. Roberta Fulbright of Fayetteville, Arkansas, owner and publisher of the *Daily Democrat*. At this time she was a Caraway supporter, writing, "Our woman senator is blazing a new trail and a glowing one," in her "As I See It" column. Later she supported her son J. William Fulbright in his 1944 race to succeed Sen. Caraway.
4. Monticello, Arkansas, attorney, chairman of the Democratic State Committee, and supporter of Gov. Parnell.

JUNE 4, 1932

Convinced of the paramount necessity of a balanced budget, the Senate takes up the so-called economy bill, designed to reduce substantially the salaries of all federal employees. Sen. Caraway consistently votes with a minority attempting to exempt low-income employees from the proposed reductions.

Finally voted on pay cuts. I tried to help all I could. No success.

JUNE 5, 1932

Sunday worked all day. Paul confined to Barracks. Red scare.[1] Much talk.

1. By this date, twenty-five thousand unemployed and penniless World War I veterans had descended upon Washington demanding immediate payment of the soldiers' bonus authorized by the Adjusted Compensation Act of 1924 but not due for payment until 1945. Although the official leaders of the so-called Bonus Army were militantly opposed to the communist minority in their midst, some within the administration persisted in characterizing all of the veterans as radicals, revolutionaries, and reds.

JUNE 6, 1932

Mr. Couch—Johnson & Mr. Pete Couch[1] came to see me. Many nasty letters. I have voted crossly all day.

1. Harvey Couch (see journal entry January 11, 1932, n.2) with his son Johnson and his brother and associate Charles Peter Couch.

JUNE 9, 1932

Little journal I have neglected you maybe because I've been so sleepy and much because I have[1]

1. The fading out and temporary cessation of the journal is discussed in the introduction.

JANUARY 3, 1934

After a whirlwind of legislative response to President Roosevelt's recovery programs in the First Session of the Seventy-third Congress from March to June 1933, the Second Session is now officially convening, and Sen. Caraway is obviously delighted with the pageantry of the occasion and the companionship of her colleagues.

On the job. Many people in all wanting to see the show. Am very favorably impressed by Sam Rorex.[1] He is likable. President appeared in person. I walked over to House with Sen. Costigan of Colorado.[2] The President made an attractive speech but surprisingly he seemed nervous. Spoke to Miss Perkins.[3] Ickes[4] there looking bullheaded as usual. It was nice to see all the men glad handing around.

1. Sam Rorex of Russellville had been an aide to Gov. Parnell, an attorney for the State Banking Department, and a member of the Arkansas Tax Commission. He made an unsuccessful race for the seat Rep. Heartsill Ragon vacated in 1933 to take a federal judgeship and shortly after was named a United States Attorney.
2. Sen. Edward P. Costigan (D-Colo.).
3. Frances Perkins, Secretary of Labor. Although widely referred to as "Miss Perkins," she was in fact the wife of Paul Wilson.
4. Harold L. Ickes, Secretary of the Interior.

JANUARY 4, 1934

Senate met for short time. Adjourned until Monday.

JANUARY 5, 1934

Garrett called home because of death of father.

JANUARY 14, 1934

Bob home from West Point. When I got his telegram that he was found[1] I did not get to sleep all night.

1. "Found" is West Point parlance for failed. Bob took intensive math courses during the summer of 1934 preparing to reenter West Point that fall but was killed in a horseback-riding accident while visiting relatives in Newbern, Tennessee, on July 31.

JANUARY 25, 1934

While the Senate debates the proposed gold reserve act, which Sen. Warren R. Austin (R-Vt.) opposes as an unconstitutional delegation of the congressional power to regulate the value of money, Sen. Caraway expresses some cynical thoughts on the artificiality of her public stature.

Made a speech to Sen. Wagner's alma mater.[1] Not much of a speech. Sen. Austin making a speech. He has gradually taken on the speaking mannerisms of Artie[2] of Ind. In talk to school I recited to them how little claim to fame I have as "the only woman senator." Sen. Pope[3] introduced two women from his state who said they looked down on Senate and wondered who I was and when he told them they were much pleased to meet. Of what things is fame made? "Thank God I too shall die" —

1. Sen. Robert F. Wagner (D-N.Y.) graduated from the City College of New York; no record of Sen. Caraway's remarks can be located.
2. Sen. Arthur R. Robinson (R-Ind.).
3. Sen. James P. Pope (D-Idaho).

MARCH 24, 1934

Sen. Caraway expresses support for President Roosevelt and Sen. Huey Long, both of whom she feels are being treated unfairly by some of her colleagues.

This journal continues to be neglected while we wrangle over patronage, St. Lawrence Waterway Treaty, Philippine Independence liberally interspersed with cries from Robinson of Indiana that the President of the U.S. is a murderer. Air mail contract cancellation being the order for wholesale murder of Army Fliers. No one who sat in the contempt proceedings against McCracken, Col. Britten and the two employees can blame the Department for cancellation of contracts so plainly obtained by fraud.[1] But of all the spectacles the attitude of the Senate in regard to Sen. Long's personal objections to D. D. Moore was one of the most indefensible.[2] Personal animosity of the older members of this body to one they surely deem an upstart. The chance to satisfy personal spleen puts the Senate in no admirable light.

1. Revelations of widespread fraud in contracts for airmail service prompted cancellation of certain commercial contracts and temporary substitution of army aviators, ten of whom were subsequently killed in crashes. On this basis, Sen. Arthur Robinson (R-Ind.), one of Roosevelt's most persistent critics, charges the president with having murdered the aviators.

2. Despite Sen. Huey Long's vehement objections (which under the long-standing custom of senatorial courtesy are usually sufficient to kill a nomination of someone from the objecting senator's state), the Senate Finance Committee recommended confirmation of Daniel D. Moore to be Collector of Internal Revenue for the Louisiana district.

MARCH 28, 1934

President Roosevelt, who received unswerving support from Sen. Caraway on such controversial measures as the Agricultural Adjustment Act, Social Security, the Tennessee Valley Authority, and the World Court, was apparently concerned enough about her support of the St. Lawrence Waterway Treaty to use heavy-handed pressure, which she resents. She is even more provoked by a continuing controversy over patronage between herself and her colleague Sen. Joe Robinson, who is now majority leader and hence has far more influence over appointments than she. She is most provoked, however, over her chauvinistic treatment by Attorney General Homer Cummings. This last entry also reiterates her apparently increasing skepticism about the personal rewards of public service.

Here on March 28th 1934 I want to inscribe in this journal the account of the only time the Pres. has talked to me in the interest of any measure that was at all close in the Senate. The St. Lawrence Waterway Treaty.[1] He called me up the evening before the vote was taken—and instead of asking me as a personal favor or for the good of the Country to vote for the treaty he made a covert threat to veto a little personal bill namely to exempt Little Rock

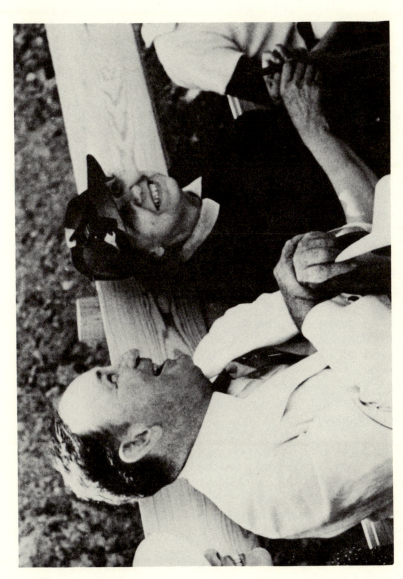

Hattie Caraway with Sen. Joseph T. Robinson. Arkansas History Commission.

College from the payment of $1400 loss to war department for materials destroyed while the College was given over to the use of the R.O.T.C.[2]

So many things to annoy come up at all times. The patronage controversy between Joe and me reached another climax—wherein separate recommendations had to go in for the District Attorney for Eastern Dist. of Ark. I was scheduled to go home on Friday. So on Mon. we got busy on appointments for me to see, personally, Farley, The Pres., and the Attorney General.[3] Farley was as always most cordial and sympathetic. How much real interest or influence he has I do not know. Anyway I left him with the feeling that he was most friendly to my desire to name at least one friend to a place of importance. The President was, as always, courteous and told me a story of the Sen's from Ky[4] wanting to name Minister to Panama.

It seems that we will say Mr. M. one time min. to Panama[5] was anxious to hold the position again. They made a plea about his great record—ability etc. The President asked if they were familiar with his record and was assured it was absolutely splendid. The Pres. then drew a letter from a Panamanian friend of his from his desk and read them this extract. "My dear Mr. Pres. Please do not send "M" to us as minister. He has the record of having pinched more ladies legs at dinner parties in the 8 years he was here than any man who has ever been in Panama." One of the Senators was teacher of a Bible Class so his confusion may be imagined. I told him I had met the gentleman and had always heard he was quite "a ladies man." Later I found that "M" had been one of my son's law instructors and his subject was *domestic relations*. Too bad I didn't have that knowledge when the President told me this story. I told him much about my candidate and he advised me to see Homer Cummings. I saw Mr. Cummings. He was nice—sympathetic—but insisted that Joe and I get together. That is always to give him his own way. Anybody can agree with Joe who will let him name all the first places.

The one thing that broke my heart in that interview was the Attorney General suggested that should my man fail to get the place that I at least am "having the fun of being the Senator." If there is any fun in being a Senator I've yet to find it. My idea of this job is to do my level best to represent the people of my State, not only in matters of legislation but in all matters where I can be of service. Enough of this. These are all things everyone meets face to face in this job, but we are supposed to count it all fun because we are elected to *high* office.

1. President Roosevelt was urging ratification of a treaty for joint U.S.—Canadian development of the St. Lawrence River. His concern about Sen. Caraway's vote was probably based on Sen. Long's denunciation of the treaty as a first step toward internationalization of all United States waterways, including the Mississippi River.

2. See journal entry for March 10, 1932, n. 4.

3. James A. Farley, President Roosevelt's campaign manager and Postmaster General; President Roosevelt; Attorney General Homer Cummings.

4. Sen. Alben W. Barkley and Sen. Marvel M. Logan, both Democrats.

5. John Glover South of Frankfort, Kentucky, served as envoy extraordinary and minister plenipotentiary to Panama from 1921 to 1929.

Bibliography

PRIMARY SOURCES

DOCUMENTS

Congressional Directory. Washington, D.C.: U.S. Government Printing Office, 1912-1936.
Congressional Record. Washington, D.C.: U.S. Government Printing Office, 1931-1934.

INTERVIEWS AND CORRESPONDENCE

Barrett, Joe C., personal interview, Jonesboro, Arkansas, June 22, 1978.
Brewer, Joe, telephone interview, July 5, 1978.
Caraway, Brig. Gen. Forrest and Mrs., letter, July 27, 1978.
Caraway, Lewes, personal interview, Washington, D.C., July 10, 1978.
Caraway, Lt. Gen. and Mrs. Paul Wyatt, personal interview, July 9, 1978.
Hays, Hon. Brooks, telephone interview, July 10, 1978.
Martin, Joe N., personal interview, June 26, 1978.
McMath, Sidney S., telephone interview, June 28, 1978.
Miller, Judge John E., letter, June 13, 1978.
Penix, Bill, personal interview, Jonesboro, Arkansas, June 23, 1978.
Ramey, Anne Hawthorne, telephone interview, June 23, 1978.
Renfro, Susan, telephone interview, July 11, 1978.
Troutt, Fred, personal interview, Jonesboro, Arkansas, June 23, 1978.
Wells, John, telephone interview, June 8, 1978.

NEWSPAPERS

Arkansas Democrat.
Arkansas Gazette.
Jonesboro Daily Tribune.
Jonesboro Sun.
Memphis Commercial Appeal.
New York Times.
Northwest Arkansas Times.
Washington Post.

SPECIAL COLLECTIONS

Arkansas History Commission, Little Rock, Arkansas. Caraway file.
Arkansas History Commission, Little Rock, Arkansas. Pulaski County
    Democratic Central Committee Scrapbook, 1931-1950.
University of Arkansas, Fayetteville, Arkansas. Special Collections. Hattie
    Wyatt Caraway Papers.

SECONDARY SOURCES

Adams, Travis Martin. "The Arkansas Congressional Delegation During
    the New Deal, 1933-36." Master's thesis, Vanderbilt University,
    1962.
Chamberlin, Hope. *A Minority of Members: Women in the U. S. Congress.*
    New York: Praeger Publishers, 1973.
Connally, Senator Tom. *My Name Is Tom Connally.* New York: Thomas
    Y. Crowell, 1954.
Creel, George. "The Woman Who Holds Her Tongue." *Collier's,* Septem-
    ber 18, 1937, pp. 22, 55.
Deutsch, Hermann B. "Hattie and Huey." *Saturday Evening Post,* October
    15, 1932, pp. 6-7, 88-90, 92.
Drury, Allen. *A Senate Journal, 1943-1945.* New York: Da Capo Press, 1972.
Duffus, R. L. "A Woman Treads New Paths As Senator." *New York Times
    Magazine,* January 24, 1932.
Frankovic, Kathleen A. "Sex and Voting in the U.S. House of Representa-
    tives: 1961-1975." *American Politics Quarterly* 5 (July 1977): 315-
    330.
Hicks, John D. *Republican Ascendancy, 1921-1933.* New York: Harper
    and Row, 1963.
Karnig, A., and Walter, O. "Elections of Women to City Councils." *Social
    Science Quarterly* 57 (March 1976): 605-613.

Kennan, William R. "Senator Hattie Caraway: A Study in Rhetorical Efficacy." Master's thesis, University of Arkansas, 1976.

Key, V. O., Jr. *Southern Politics*. New York: Alfred A. Knopf, 1950.

Kincaid, Diane D. "Over His Dead Body: A Positive Perspective on Widows in the U.S. Congress." *Western Political Quarterly* 31 (March 1978): 96-104.

Kirkpatrick, Jeane J. *Political Woman*. New York: Basic Books, 1974.

"Last of the First." *Time*, August 7, 1944, p. 19.

Lee, Marcia. "Toward Understanding Why Few Women Hold Public Office: Factors Affecting the Participation of Women in Local Politics." In *A Portrait of Marginality: The Political Behavior of the American Woman*, edited by Marianne Githens and Jewel L. Prestage, pp. 118-138. New York: David McKay, 1977.

Leuchtenburg, William E. *Franklin D. Roosevelt and the New Deal, 1932-1940*. New York: Harper and Row, 1963.

Martin, Thomas. *Dynasty: The Longs of Louisiana*. New York: G. P. Putnam's, 1960.

Mears, William Curtis. "L. S. (Sharpe) Dunaway." *Arkansas Historical Quarterly* 13 (1954): 77-85.

Moffat, Mary Jane, and Painter, Charlotte. *Revelations: Diaries of Women*. New York: Random House, 1975.

Patterson, James T. *Congressional Conservatism and the New Deal: The Growth of the Conservative Coalition in Congress, 1933-1939*. Lexington: University of Kentucky Press, 1967.

Paxton, Annabel. *Women in Congress*. Richmond, Va.: Dietz Press, 1945.

Pownell, Sharon. "Senator Hattie Caraway." *Craighead County Historical Quarterly*, April 1, 1975, pp. 3-11.

Schlesinger, Arthur M., Jr. *The Crisis of the Old Order, 1919-33*. Boston: Houghton Mifflin, 1956.

Scott, Anne Firor. *The Southern Lady: From Pedestal to Politics, 1830-1930*. Chicago: University of Chicago Press, 1970.

Shannon, David A. *Between the Wars: America, 1919-1941*. Boston: Houghton Mifflin, 1965.

Smith, Gene. *The Shattered Dream: Herbert Hoover and the Great Depression*. New York: William Morrow, 1970.

Sneed, Betty M. "Hattie Wyatt Caraway: United States Senator, 1931-1945." Master's thesis, University of Arkansas, 1975.

Towns, Stuart. "A Louisiana Medicine Show: The Kingfish Elects an Arkansas Senator." *Arkansas Historical Quarterly* 25 (Summer 1966): 117-127.

Tucker, Ray, and Barkley, Frederick R. *Sons of The Wild Jackass*. Boston: L. C. Page & Co., 1932.

Wells, John. "Origin of the Hatch Act." *Little Rock Weekly News Review,* June 17, 1978.

Wheeler, Burton K. *Yankee From the West.* Garden City, N.Y.: Doubleday, 1962.

Whiteside, Garrett. "Watching Washington for Thirty-five Years." *Arkansas Historical Quarterly* 1 (September 1942): 235-243.

Williams, Harry Lee. *Forty Years Behind The Scenes In Arkansas Politics. An Expose of Actual Facts Presented Without Bias, Yet Pulling No Punches, While Relating Many Incidents Which Occurred Behind the Scenes in State Campaigns and in the Legislature.* Little Rock, Ark.: Parkin Printing & Stationery Co., 1949.

Williams, T. Harry. *Huey Long.* New York: Alfred A. Knopf, 1969.

Wilson, Winston P. *Harvey Couch: The Master Builder.* Nashville, Tenn.: Broadman Press, 1947.

Women State Legislators: Report from a Conference. New Brunswick, N.J.: Eagleton Institute, Center for the Study of Women in Politics, May 1973.

Young, Louise M. "Hattie Ophelia Wyatt Caraway." In *Notable American Women, 1607-1950,* edited by Edward T. James. Cambridge: Belknap Press of Harvard University Press, 1971.

Index

About the Author

Diane D. Kincaid is Political Science Instructor at the University of Arkansas. She has had articles published in *Western Political Quarterly, The School Administrator,* and *Publius, Annual Review of Federalism.*